America's 1890s Parachute Queen

Pioneer Skydiving Sensation
Miss Hazel Keyes

William D. Kalt, III

Universal-Publishers

Irvine • Boca Raton

America's 1890s Parachute Queen: Pioneer Skydiving Sensation Miss Hazel Keyes

Universal Publishers, Inc.
Irvine • Boca Raton
USA • 2022
www.Universal-Publishers.com

ISBN: 978-1-62734-412-8 (pbk.)
ISBN: 978-1-62734-413-5 (ebk.)

Front cover image: Miss Hazel Keyes posed hanging from a parachute for photos in the Trover-Cronise Studio, which produced glass negatives. (Oregon Historical Society A-886-b)

Typeset by Medlar Publishing Solutions Pvt Ltd, India
Cover design by Ivan Popov

Library of Congress Cataloging-in-Publication Data

Names: Kalt, William D., III, author.
Title: America's 1890s Parachute Queen : pioneer skydiving sensation Miss Hazel Keyes / William D. Kalt, III.
Other titles: Pioneer skydiving sensation Miss Hazel Keyes
Description: Irvine : Universal Publishers, [2022] | Includes bibliographical references.
Identifiers: LCCN 2022027170 (print) | LCCN 2022027171 (ebook) | ISBN 9781627344128 (paperback) | ISBN 9781627344135 (ebook)
Subjects: LCSH: Keyes, Hazel, 1861-1940. | Skydivers--United States--Biography. | Women in aeronautics--United States.
Classification: LCC TL751.K49 K35 2022 (print) | LCC TL751.K49 (ebook) | DDC 797.5/6092 [B]--dc23/eng/20220609
LC record available at https://lccn.loc.gov/2022027170
LC ebook record available at https://lccn.loc.gov/2022027171

America's 1890s
Parachute Queen

Table of Contents

Acknowledgments

Editors: Charity Everitt, David Devine, Sharon E. Hunt.

Generous thanks and appreciation to the men and women who aided in producing this book: Gail Kalt; Renato Rodriquez, San Diego History Center; Austin Schultz, Oregon State Archives; Natalie Brandt, State Library of Oregon; Matthew Cowan, Scott Rook, Robert Warren, Oregon Historical Society; Carol Olten, La Jolla Historical Society; Gary Carpentier (Noble Grand), and Tina Chong, International Order of Odd Fellows, Los Angeles-Golden Rule #35; Tom Schmidt, Sharlot Hall Museum.

Introduction

America's Pioneer Parachuting Queen, its "Annie Oakley of the Air," thrilled fans in a style befitting her crack shot counterpart. While never achieving Oakley's international fame, Miss Hazel Keyes drew spectators to her parachuting performances by the thousands for more than a decade. Her death-defying skydives brought her both terror and pain, but she endured to thrill the multitudes and earn fame throughout the nation. In an era where women's limited job opportunities included teacher, food server, factory worker, maid, laundry worker, dance hall/burlesque performer, and courtesan, Keyes shattered social norms and earned income well beyond her earth-bound cohort.

One finds much in yesteryear's newspapers of kings and queens, presidents, military generals, business magnates, and the supremely talented. Their accomplishments and missteps fill the headlines and provide the grist for eager journalists and spirited conversationalists across the decades. A scant few public figures whose fame glistens in the spotlight repeatedly resurface during 50 years of news-making events. Here chronicled stands one such example.

While some reporters of a century past used puffery and exaggeration to stimulate readership, much of the tenor of the events and times still emerges. These kernels of understanding often arrive draped in an eloquence of expression scarcely seen in the modern era. Given these realities, one might question whether the story herewith speaks fact or fable, despite its exacting documentation. While the beliefs, customs, and stories of a community passed on by word of mouth constitute folklore, this record takes its gist from the published versions of the day. It recounts the documented events in the life of one of the first female parachutists on America's Western frontier. As with any mortal trek upon the earth, peaks and valleys populate her timeline, often outdistancing the societal norm. Passionate, gritty, bold, indomitable, of questionable scruples at times, attractive, determined, meticulous, and mindful, Miss Hazel Keyes checked all the boxes as she took the air behind an illustrious crew of early aeronauts.

Human flight shot aloft when brothers Joseph-Michel and Jacques-Étienne Montgolfier ignited wood, straw, and old shoes beneath an alum–coated, paper-lined, sackcloth balloon. Filled with hot air, it carried the first living creatures, a sheep, a duck, and a cockerel, off the earth in a basket on September 19, 1783. Two months later,

"Machinae Novae" depicts Croatian Faust Vrancic's leap from Venice's St. Mark's Campanile's tower using his rudimentary parachute, the Homo Volans. (https://lccn.loc.gov/ 2006690488)

Jean-François Pilâtre de Rozier and Francois Laurent, marquis d'Arlandes, made the first free-flying journey beneath a Montgolfier balloon. The feat forever altered humanity's perspective and reality. No longer confined to their earthly abode, souls and spirits shot into the firmament in a parade of respect and honor for the physics that allowed hot air to rise, gravity's unretreating power, the force of air resistance, and the whims of the winds. More than a century later, balloons continued to provide humans with the surest manner of flying. Conceptualizing a leap from high in the sky bred its corollary—surviving the landing and ingenuity took varied paths. In the 9th century, inventor, astronomer, physician, chemist, engineer, and musician Abbas Ibn Firnas covered a wooden frame with feathers to create a wing-like parachute. He flew for 10 minutes and executed a smooth descent before injuring his back on the landing. Italian polymath Leonardo da Vinci drew cone-shaped linen parachutes designed to help people leap from burning buildings in the 1480s. More than a century passed before Croatian polymath Faust Vrančić (Faustio Veranzio) reportedly jumped from Venice's St. Mark's Campanile's tower in his rudimentary parachute, the *Homo Volans* (Flying Man) in 1617.

While other aerial creators might have explored parachute possibilities during the intervening years, French inventor Louis-Sébastien Lenormand earned recognition for the first parachute descent in 1783, using his rigid frame invention. His compatriot, Jean Pierre Blanchard, developed the initial soft, foldable silk parachute two years later. André-Jacques Garnerin followed, surviving the world's initial high-altitude parachute jump from a balloon at 3,200 feet in 1797.[1]

Sebastien-Louis Lenormand used a wooden framed parachute to execute a successful 4.3 meter (14-foot) leap from France's Montpellier Observatory tower in 1783. (Wikicommons, Early flight 02561u [3])

For some, leaping back to earth proved enticing—even inspiring. As famed aviator Charles A. Lindbergh would later declare, "Why force one's body from a plane to make a parachute jump? Why should man fly at all? What civilization was not founded on adventure? I believe the risks I take [jumping with a parachute] are justified by the sheer life I lead."[2]

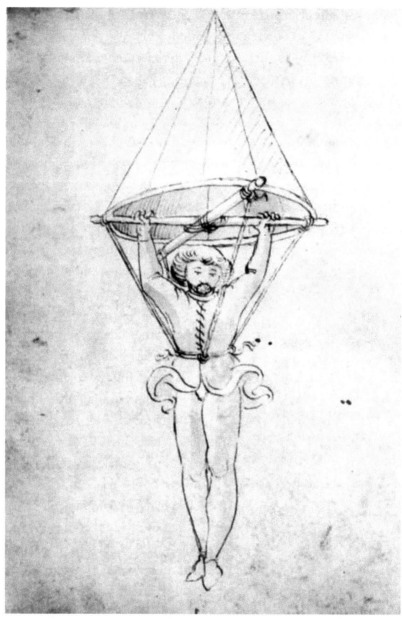

An unknown artist depicted the first parachute (above) in the 1470s, preceding Leonardo da Vinci's sketches by 13 years. Five centuries later, Brit Adrian Nicholas used da Vinci's design to leap from 10,000 feet using a 187-pound parachute. (Conical Parachute, 1470s, British Museum Add. MSS 34,113, fol. 200v.jpg)

1

Miss Hazel's Perilous Plunge

"She's a goner! What a fearful mishap! Can he save her? Will he let go?" screamed an *Arizona Republican* reporter, bringing a terrifying January 1895 Phoenix afternoon to life. "Such and many more were the horrified exclamations of spectators of the balloon ascension at the race-track yesterday afternoon as the great inflated monster soared upward."

After hot air filled her colorful balloon, Miss Hazel Keyes, seated upon a trapeze bar suspended beneath it, shouted, "All let go!" In that instant, the giant cloth bag rocketed into the heavens, snapping the cords that held her parachute to it. Shooting upward, strapped to her balloon by only one remaining cord, her parachute unfolded and engulfed her. Miss Hazel's partner in the double parachute jump, Prof. E.J. Lee, rose safely, sitting on his trapeze bar beneath his balloon.

Miss Hazel thrust her hips and legs back and forth as she tried to swing out and reach Lee and his precious

Arizona Republican, January 27, 1895

parachute. She screamed, "Don't leave me, or I am lost." Hearing her frenzied cries and seeing her entangled in the useless parachute, Professor Lee extended his leg as far as he could toward her. She clutched his calf at last and leaped from her bag. Together, they hurtled skyward, and their balloon soon looked about the size of a man, the aeronauts doll-size.

Towering now, still, the balloon soared. Prof. Lee cut the cord, releasing their single parachute from the balloon and initiating their descent. Spectators saw him suspended in a rope harness with Miss Hazel clinging to it. Approaching the ground too fast, they sailed toward the Salt River, turgid and turbulent from recent desert rainstorms. About 20 feet from the water, they both let go of the parachute. Nearly losing consciousness as she splashed into the water, Miss Hazel ripped her trunks and severely bruised her left knee. Thrashing hard against the thundering current, she battled without success to make it to shore. Two men waded into the water, hoisted her onto the back of a pony, and carried her to safety—drenched and injured. The parachute landed on the river's opposite bank near Prof. Lee, who received barely a scratch.

Declaring, "Death Grinned at Two Clinging Aeronauts," the *Republican* writer observed, "Miss Hazel Keyes and Prof. Lee survived their experience of yesterday afternoon and may yet make many a balloon ascension together. But it is doubtful if any of the spectators of their performance will ever be persuaded to make an air voyage either as passengers or principals." Many spectators spoke "of the fabulous amounts which they would scornfully refuse rather than do so. The announcement that the lady and gentleman had resolved to quit their profession forever would be a surprise to none."[3]

In truth, Miss Hazel and her life-saving partner, Prof. Lee, stood as just two of a cadre of daredevils who "rode the bag" and jumped from it for coin and glory. Leaping into the parachuting derby promised a visit to life's extremes and the tempting of fate's last straw. The sport inflamed danger's most insane passions, and parachute performances highlighted many 1890s state fairs and amusement exhibitions. From a basket suspended beneath their balloon, seated on a trapeze-style bar, or clutching an iron ring, these death-dodgers dove toward the dirt for a piece of the gate or a showman's guarantee. Birthed in the sense of what was possible, through a perspective next-to-no-one enjoyed, these early sky-jumpers spirited death along like an unruly child, whipping the air in its defiance—until they didn't.

Madame Jeanne-Geneviève Garnerin, the first woman to ascend in a balloon without a male partner, sailed above fashionably dressed spectators in this 1802 etching. (http://hdl.loc.gov/loc.pnp/ppmsca.02548)

2

Not One a Shrinking Violet: Chute Yes, I'll Jump!

Captain Thomas S. Baldwin made the first recognized United States' parachute leap from his balloon at Golden Gate Park on January 30, 1887. Sitting on a small seat, holding tight to an iron ring with his parachute dangling beneath him, Baldwin earned $1.00 for each foot he rose in his balloon. After reaching sufficient height, he pulled a

Early inventors experimented with burning sulfuric acid and iron filings in a barrel to make hydrogen gas and fill a balloon in this illustration by Faujas-de-St.-Fond, (Barthélemy). Later aeronauts used naphtha, alcohol, or gasoline to fuel their fires. ("Plate 3: Filing the Balloon with Hydrogen Gas." In Description des Expériences de la Machine Aérostatique De MM. De Montgolfier. Paris, France: Cuchet, 1783) https:// digital.sciencehistory.org/works/3197xm10p.

"rip panel" attached to the balloon to release the parachute, which filled with a rush of air. Baldwin jumped off his seat and floated to safety, commencing America's fascination with the parachuting spectacle. Promoters and aerialists who recognized the public's waning interest in simple balloon flights soon brought forth these more dangerous stunts to thrill onlookers.[4]

Early aeronauts ignited a mixture of sulfuric acid and iron filings to create hydrogen gas and fill their balloons. The process consumed several hours, and the craft proved challenging to control on the descent. With the adoption of "smokies," simple, lower-cost cloth bags filled with heated air, balloons took less time to inflate and shot up to 1,000 feet in a flash. Adding excitement for entertainment-starved crowds, it meant many more thrillseekers could try vaulting from their balloon with a parachute. Historian Tom D. Crouch notes, "Suddenly in the 1880s and early 1890s, semi-suicidal daredevils seemed to be leaping over every small town in America, often with disastrous results."[5]

With madcaps filling American skies, some aeronauts drew massive crowds to their skydiving performances. Requiring steel nerves, iron hands, a forgiving body, instantaneous reactions, good vision, and a short memory, the terrifying sky-plunging affair attracted women as well as men. While females comprised only a small percentage of parachute jumpers, those who entered the game shone as brightly as their male colleagues. France's Jeanne-Geneviève Garnerin earned credit as the first woman to execute a solo parachute jump in 1799. She completed many descents while touring with her husband André-Jacques, who invented the frameless parachute. Her niece, Elisa Garnerin, joined in and completed 39 professional descents between 1815 and 1836.

Sophie Blanchard, the initial professional female aerialist, first piloted a balloon solo in 1805. She entertained crowds, including Napoleon Bonaparte, in more than 60 ascensions following her husband Jean-Pierre Blanchard's 1809 death. Sophie specialized in night flights before she perished in a fiery 1819 ballooning accident. The first female parachute jumper in Los Angeles, Jeanette Van Tassel, proclaimed in 1888, "I ain't exactly a bird nor an angel, but it's just about what I imagine[d] the sensation of flying is. It was beautiful! It is only a question of nerve." In the 1890s, Germany's Katharina "Käthe" Paulus earned fame making 165 jumps and inventing the first collapsible parachute.[6]

When Miss Hazel Keyes joined the skydiving circuit, she gained fame across the United States for her parachuting exploits. However, few modern-day publications reference the courageous woman.

Entitled "Le Ballon Captif," this illustration depicts a "captive balloon." Designed by Henry Giffard and exhibited in 1867, it remained tethered to the earth in a city plaza throughout the exhibition. (http://hdl.loc.gov/loc.pnp/ ppmsca.02290)

Richard T. Read and David Rambow describe her act in *Hydrogen and Smoke: A Survey of Lighter-Than-Air Flight in South Dakota Prior to World War I*. Gary B. Fogel and Craig S. Harwood mention Keyes in their *Quest for Flight: John J. Montgomery and the Dawn of Aviation in the West*. In addition, ballooninghistory.com's "Who's Who in Ballooning" devotes one paragraph to her aerial exploits.[7]

Why Professor?

Much as 19th-century newspapers often referred to titans of industry, banking, and other fields with the title Colonel, so aeronauts and band leaders wore the moniker, Professor. Neither required the commonly associated military or educational credentials.

The Smoke Balloon

Cutting-edge technology at the time, the average "smokie" stood about 60 feet tall and 28 feet in diameter. It contained three sections: a double-thickness "cap" at the top to prevent it from igniting; a "midsection," which held about 40 "gores," or strips of muslin soaked in a solution of glue, water, soda, alum, whiting, and salt to fill its pores; and, an eight-foot-in-diameter iron ring to form its "mouth" at the bottom. Sturdy cords strapped the balloon's midsection to the ring, and cables or a trapeze bar hung from it for the parachutist during ascent. *(Richard T. Read and David Rambow, Hydrogen and Smoke: A Survey of Lighter-Than-Air Flight in South Dakota Prior to World War I. South Dakota Historical Society Press, Pierre, vol. 18(3): Fall 1988. P. 135–136). (https://www.sdhspress.com/journal/south-dakota-history-18-3/hydrogen-and-smoke-a-survey-of-lighter-than-air-flight-in-south-dakota-prior-to-world-war-i)*

Käthe Paulus (1868–1935) posed atop a basket beneath her balloon in this ca. 1890 image. Paulus employed the parachute she invented with Paul Lattemann. Folded into a knapsack and secured with a breakcord, the parachute released when the jumper left the balloon, and the cord snapped.

(1890 Fotomontage 3256644 1450825047-e1450825180)

Miss Hazel Keyes posed in her regalia before a November 1893 Salem, Oregon, skydiving performance. (Oregon Historical Society [OHS] A-886)

3

Who Is This Flying Phenom?

Miss Hazel Keyes entered the public eye well before her parachuting career and remained long after its conclusion. Her forceful nature and self-assuredness would endure throughout her almost 80 years. Born Martha H. Horton in 1861, her mother, Mary Adeline Redmond, worked "keeping house," while her father, William Horton, toiled as a farm laborer in Los Nietos Township, California. The family's estate, valued at just $150 in 1870 ($3,132 in 2021), suggests a subsistence-type lifestyle. Though few facts emerge regarding her childhood, Miss Hazel moved to Oregon around 15, where she and Joseph A. Keyes celebrated the birth of their first son, Henry C. Keyes, in Portland on October 24, 1876. The couple married two years later, and she used the name "Mattie" Redmond (her mother's maiden name) when the couple wed on December 26, 1878, in Red Bluff, Tehama County, California. In addition to son Henry, the union produced daughter Mary Hazel and sons Joseph A. and Edward S. "Eddie" Keyes. Mattie (Miss Hazel) married three times during her tumultuous life, and her amorous escapades wreaked havoc. The frequency of her documented entanglements prompts conjecture as to those that might have gone unreported.[8]

Rage followed fury in August 1886, when her husband Joseph suspected betrayal. Kisses, hugs, brief touches on the arm, intimate sexual relations, or just furtive glances? What, at last, pushed Joseph over the line remains unclear. He filed a lawsuit declaring that his boss, Edward James Jeffery, a married father of two, had "alienated from him the affections of his better half." Joseph asserted that the couple's marital relationship lacked the loving affection he once enjoyed due to Jeffery's actions. "His grief and indignation are so intense it will take $15,000 to put him in good humor again," reported Salem's *Oregon Daily Statesman*. However, when the case came to court, Joseph's attorney moved to dismiss the suit with "no reason assigned." Whether true reconciliation or simple mutual tolerance guided the marriage henceforth went unreported. However, still referred to as his wife, Miss Hazel would come to Joseph's legal aid five years later.[9]

Miss Hazel's husband, Joseph Keyes, claimed that dashing Edward James Jeffery steered his wife's loving affections away from their marriage. (www.fndagrave.com, Friends of Riverview #95857783)

America's future Parachuting Queen made her next newspaper appearance in September 1886, when she battled "improper advances." The traumatic incident clearly demonstrated the steely determination and fearless approach to a confrontation that would forever mark her life. Trouble began when landlord Perry G. Baker arrived to collect the rent at the Keyes' Clay Street and Seventh Street home in Portland. When Baker made unwanted sexual advances in addition to his demands for the rent, Miss Hazel stopped him. Rejected, Baker smashed her in the mouth and on the side of her head with his clenched fist. A passerby reported the assault to Judge Tuttle, and a nearby reporter rushed to the scene. There, he found Mattie Keyes (Miss Hazel) "moaning and crying, her upper lip cut and swollen and a bruise on the right side of her head."[10]

Mattie filed suit seeking $5,000, but failed to appear at the trial and forfeited her court costs. She complicated her case when police charged her with larceny for stealing a silver watch from her attorney, Mary Leonard. Brought to trial, Mattie declared that she had given the timepiece to a young man to "regulate," adjust, and set and had never intended to keep it. To her good fortune, Justice Stuart found that the "prosecution failed to show that Mrs. Keyes had converted the property to her own use" and dismissed the case.[11]

Indefatigable, Mattie took Baker back to court the following June, suing this time for $2,000. Her complaint specified, "The defendant willfully, maliciously, and violently assaulted" her and "struck her several heavy blows on the face, cut her lip, [and] injured one of her eyes." He "seized her by the neck while he was administering blows," tore her clothes off, and "threw her with violence against a tree, thereby bruising seriously" her side. Further, she "was made sick for a considerable length of time [and] was compelled to employ a physician at the expense of $20 and suffered great mental and physical anguish." Dr. Mackenzie testified that her injuries required three weeks of treatment. The landlord admitted hitting her but claimed self-defense, stating that she "tongue-lashed him." Policemen Collins and Stuart testified that "Mrs. Keyes' character was bad"; after all her pain and trouble, Mattie recovered only $50.[12]

Grander adventures lay ahead for Miss Hazel Keyes, however. After her husband Joseph began skydiving, she took parachute training from Oregon's renowned Professor Frank P. Hagal in the late 1880s. Hagal also instructed James J. Romig, whose fiery love affair with Keyes filled with spectacle. Those nearby might have witnessed the sizzling sparks of their first eye contact, heard the flush of passion's rushing breath, and felt the heat of their first sumptuous touch. Thus ensued a brilliant love affair, which might well have begun in the air and stretched the bounds of social convention in a myriad of manners. Such temporally transcendent love lies deep within the soul of humanity, reflected in the verse of great poets and the works of fine painters. Its worldly manifestation might not always make that grade.[13]

The Keyes family moved to Oakland, California, where heartache filled their Sixteenth Street home when pneumonia took one-and-one-half-year-old Mary Hazel Keyes. The grief-laden family buried their daughter in Saint Mary's Cemetery on January 18, 1890. The lung-ravaging disease also appears to have grounded Joseph Keyes' parachuting career. After struggling to feed her family for several months, Mattie returned to Oregon. She first took the air to earn a living as the aeronaut Miss Hazel Keyes through a series of events.[14]

The sequence began when her training partner, Romig, ordered a new balloon for an August 1890 double parachute jump in Uppertown Astoria, Oregon. After Romig took ill and his partner, Miss Bertha Onzalo, backed out, Bertha's husband jumped instead. Attempting only his third parachute leap, Arthur Cosgrove, 28, fueled himself with alcohol before the skydive. Bidding his goodbyes and kissing his small boy, the local variety theater manager refused to strap himself to his parachute. Rising with the balloon, Arthur cut the parachute free and held on until he floated down to about 150 feet above the turf. Then, he let go and dropped to a ghastly death, smashing onto the paved street in front of East Portland, Oregon's First Presbyterian Church.[15]

Following Cosgrove's appalling death, sources revealed that a tortuous parachuting love triangle precipitated his demise. Cosgrove believed himself cuckolded by parachuting performer Professor C.P. Redmond, who had made several ascensions with his wife. The idea that his betrothed's "affections were centered in Redmond preyed" on Arthur's mind. After Redmond landed on top of a 200-foot-tall tree and tumbled to his death, Cosgrove decided to kill himself. Later reports spoke of Miss Bertha Onzalo's diminished interest in the parachuting gambit.[16]

With 76 ascensions to his credit, Prof. Romig needed a partner for his double-parachute caper, and Miss Hazel Keyes made her first reported public balloon ascension and leap with him at Gervais, Oregon, on August 31, 1890. News accounts, however, mistakenly billed her as Miss Lottie Keys. Miss Hazel and the Prof. repeated their feat 10 days later at French Prairie. The pair electrified Oregon crowds with several more double parachute jumps of a "most sensational character."[17]

Asked by a reporter whether parachuting had "been a lifelong calling," Miss Hazel clarified, "Oh, no! My husband's health failed him, and I found it necessary to do something more lucrative than nursing. I am a trained nurse by profession. As he was a professional aeronaut, I had gathered quite an interest and knowledge of the business. I determined to enter his field and win, in a rapid way, the income necessary for the schooling of my three children, the maintenance of the family, and the added expense of his illness. I have succeeded amply in my undertaking." When her husband's condition "greatly improved, she [had] no special desire to relinquish the business," confirmed the sky flyer.[18]

4

An Aerial Mystique: America's Cavalcade of Crazy

The parachuting dynamic excited both its practitioners and throngs of witnesses eager for death-defying entertainment. Thrill-loving performers fed a passion for extreme jeopardy to play the "just might die" card and risk a smashing termination in hopes of inspiring the masses to ante up their coin. Many onlookers paid for the chance of a sensational, maybe fatal, accident that would make their outlay "worth the price" and provide them with "a damn good story to tell." Watching from the ground yielded no opportunity to affect an outcome, yet spectators clung to the operation's every move.

Each balloon ascent and parachute plunge provided a unique unfolding of danger-filled challenges. Almost all produced their desired bated-breath crowds with hearts in throats and pulses racing. From igniting the naphtha, alcohol, or other fuel to build a blaze and heat air for filling the balloon, to keeping the giant bag from lifting off prematurely, to releasing the balloon on the aeronaut's command, to its safely escaping the support poles used to hold it, peril lurked. A safe climb into the clouds while retaining hold of the balloon's cords or seated on a trapeze bar then tested the ascensionist. Wind gusts that drove the parachute in unwanted directions might have also plagued the aeronaut's ascent, pushing the balloon far from the intended landing spot.

The ability to guide the balloon away from buildings, trees, and other obstacles proved crucial.

Slicing the rope to release the parachute from the balloon provided another chance for inopportune happenstance, such as the parachute's failure to fill with air or the cords supporting the aeronaut breaking. Earthly impact introduced a unique new dimension. The relative firmness of the surface, the speed at collision, and body position at initial contact all played critical roles in the parachutist's ability to walk away from the adventure unscathed, injured but ambulatory, maimed for life, or not at all. The pluses and minuses of the decision to parachute again might have oft come to mind for these reckless plummeting pioneers.

A scribe at *The St. Paul Globe* captured the 1890s parachute performer's aura and status: "Often the parachute jumper is billed as a marvelous and thrilling free feature. He is a daring and spectacular fellow. Some persons would call him foolhardy. He is a greater drawing card than the free street parade, with the funny clown in the pony cart and the musical calliope. He takes great risks and demands big pay. Sometimes he receives $100 [$3,368 in 2021] or more for a single performance or aerial flight. It is a perilous business he follows. People flock to see his aerial gymnastics, fearing that he may be killed and that they will be so unfortunate as to miss the grewsome [sic] sight."[19]

Frequent deaths marked parachuting shows as they gained prominence in the 1890s. News stories filled with statements such as "tangled in the balloon's guy ropes," "trapped on a church spire," and "ballast striking the parachute in mid-air." Burning balloons, losing one's hold, and collapsing parachutes added to the statistics. One news account captured the moment of peak eyewitness ecstasy and terror as Miss Annie Harkness hurtled almost a mile to her death in August 1891: "There was a dreadful hush like the silence of death. The parachute had closed and, with its human burden, was falling with frightful velocity. Then, the silence was broken by the shrieks of fainting women, of children wailing and crying, and men turning away their faces from the awful sight. Faster and faster descended the parachute. More intense and terrible

THE INEVITABLE!

Gertie Carmo, the Parachutiste Meets Death at Detroit.

She Falls a Distance of 250 Feet Breaking Every Bone in Her Body.

Detroit's Gertie Carmo, 22, parachuted to her end in a sulfur marsh at the Cincinnati, Ohio 1892 Exposition when her balloon struck an electrical pole. (Akron Daily Democrat [Ohio], September 17, 1892)

became the strain upon the madly excited crowd as, horror-stricken, it stood waiting for the fearful end. Suddenly there struck upon the ear a dull, sickening sound. The end had come. A life had gone out in the midst of pleasure."[20]

Mortality greeted parachutists in a fascinating smorgasbord of deadly maladies. In one year, 26 parachuters died, and 40 received serious injuries during a 28-week season. One scribe wrote, "Hardly a day has passed that press dispatches have not announced the death or fatal accident to some daring aeronaut." Prof. H.F. Vandergrift, 25, drowned in the Chattahoochee River when his balloon exploded before 12,000 witnesses at Columbus, Georgia, and the ropes of his parachute encircled him. Sparks from a nearby mill fire set Prof. Samuel Black's parachute ablaze at St. Louis' 1890 Independence Day celebration. Black plummeted "through space at a frightful speed," and observers found his corpse disfigured. Prof. John Hogan lost his grip on the parachute before 30,000 horrified spectators at Detroit,

Michigan. He fell almost 1/2 mile and slammed onto a wooden sidewalk, shattering it. Sixteen-year-old Tillie Serbern succumbed on her initial parachute jump at Anderson, Indiana, when the ropes of her balloon proved rotten and snapped. Authorities arrested the balloon's owner and the show's manager on charges of manslaughter. "This end is in store for some of the numerous kid aeronauts who persist in giving their parents heart disease by their persistent aerial flights," declared one Indiana scribe.[21]

A strange yet understandable phenomenon accompanied some parachuting fatalities. Spectators who located aeronauts that hit the ground feet-first reported their bodies driven into the earth. In one case, Bozard Balloon Company employee Geo. B. Anderson created a 14-inch-deep hole in the Kansas soil. Professor Edward Hope established the reported record with his tragic 1892 fall from a half-mile above St. Paul, Minnesota. After his chute failed to expand, the professor plunged at a terrifying rate and landed in a marsh with such speed that it drove him 12 feet into the mud. Men dug a full hour to recover his body.[22]

While many relished parachuting's theatrics, outcry against the inhumanity of taking such risks for money came in a rush. A *Scranton Tribune* editorial screamed, "So long as people encourage balloon ascensions by financial inducements, there will be no end to the death list of the parachute victims. The morbid public is responsible for these homicides." A Grand Rapids, Michigan *Telegram-Herald* writer added, "The parachute is trying to rival the [railroad] grade crossing as a death trap."[23]

Chicago Tribune, April 25, 1897

Shock and terror play out on the faces of the crowd in this St. Louis Dispatch *artist's image of an aeronaut plunging helplessly to the ground. One chap reaches to catch the performer.* (St. Louis Dispatch, *August 29, 1890)*

A Deadly Game

Britain's Robert Cocking first proved the mortal danger of parachute jumping on July 24, 1837. An enormous crowd gathered at London's Vauxhall Gardens to watch the 61-year-old landscape painter and amateur scientist with no skydiving experience test his experimental parachute. Vibrantly adorned with a glowing, emerald-green scroll of laurel and other flashy embellishments, sections of sturdy Irish linen stitched together into a circle hung suspended under Charles Green's *Royal Nassau* balloon. Attached at the top to a 107-foot-circumference ring of two-inch soldered copper tubes supported by thin wooden ribs, the cloth culminated in a small ring with Cocking's four-foot-deep basket tethered beneath it.

Confident, Cocking strode about observing the balloon's preparation and answering questions "with great urbanity and cheerfulness." The scheme's danger grew when the parachute's large upper ring broke in three places, and workers repaired it with only wooden lath and string. After Cocking enjoyed a final glass of wine with friends, an uproarious "huzza" erupted, and the entire contraption shot aloft. Cocking's parachute performed to perfection for about 10 seconds before dropping from view into a cloud. Appearing beneath it, craft and cargo remained steady for another 40–50 seconds before the parachute's upper ring collapsed about a mile above the turf. The affair crashed to earth near Tiger's Head Lee, ending the gentleman Robert Cocking and his ill-fated experiment. *(The Observer* [London], July 30, 1837, "Particulars of the Ascent—Descent of the Parachute—Melancholy Catastrophe"; https://iiif.wellcomecollection.org/image/V0040870/full/full/0/default.jpg)

the **NASSAU BALLOON** with
The Parachute as it appended.

Mr. **COCKING.**

the **PARACHUTE** as it
descended by which Mr Cocking
lost his life July 24 1837

5

Like a Cardinal Venus in a Sea of Emerald

Amid the cascade of death that engulfed her profession, Miss Hazel Keyes traveled the West, staging parachuting exhibitions. A mid-November 1890 flight at San Francisco's Baker Beach marked one of her early leaps. On the western edge of the city's Presidio, a raging fire heated air to fill her huge, colorful cloth balloon for an escape from gravity's chokehold. Soon, the massive bag strained to break free from the grip of well-muscled men who held it back. When the hissing monster took its fill, Miss Hazel gave the "let go all" cry, and her crew cut loose sandbags, which weighed the balloon down, and released its tie ropes. As it jetted skyward, the lass, dazzling in her scarlet attire, erupted in a triumphant, "Whoop!"[24]

Miss Hazel rose to 3,000 feet, sliced the cord securing her to the balloon, jumped free, and began a gentle descent as her parachute caught air. "If Miss Keyes had been allowed a week in which to pick out the point at which she was again to rejoin her native element [earth], she could not have selected a more auspicious spot, for it was on soft soil in a cabbage patch of the Italian garden near the railroad," wrote a columnist. "Just before touching the ground, she gracefully freed herself from the parachute and landed safely on her feet." One of the day's

2,000 earth-bound admirers rhapsodized, "She looked like a cardinal Venus descending into a sea of emerald."[25]

Miss Hazel moved on to perform with Professor Romig at the Oakland Trotting Park in February 1891. All went well with their flights, but young toughs stole their balloon, requiring police assistance to recover the cloth affair. Plans next called for a St. Patrick's Day round of ascensions at Eureka, California. Perhaps no town in her career proved more delighted to see Miss Hazel perform than Eureka. An effusive journalist recounted the electrifying nature and impact of her March 1891 visit to the small town. "Our citizens, with beaming countenances and souls overflowing with gratitude," wrote the reporter, "take each other by the hand and in one breath exclaim, 'Did you see the balloon?'" Townspeople concurred "that the ascension was the greatest event in the annals of Eureka, if not the United States. [It] will form a favorite topic of conversation around the family fireside." Miss Hazel's name "henceforth [will] be associated and mentioned with the names of other illustrious personages in the history of Humboldt County."[26]

Eureka resident Dan McGinty held a different view and aimed the only documented criticism of its kind at Miss Hazel during her brilliant career. Describing her as "a vision of female loveliness flitting amongst the crowd," McGinty nevertheless impugned her character after winds mounted, and she declared it too dangerous to go aloft. McGinty claimed, "The audience was much displeased, and all went home, crying 'fake,' 'bilk,' etc." The aerialists' troubles grew as most of Eureka looked on four days after their triumphant performance that received the rave review. A battle between Prof. Romig and Miss Hazel over who would ascend spun out of control in loud bursts of profanity, and the balloon flew off without either one aboard. Things worsened after her helpers released the balloon, and it lifted a piece of timber that almost smashed a small boy. "Thus, the balloon-loving public was duped again," declared McGinty. "Like all the rest of the fakirs [sic] that come here, she managed to beat the public."[27]

Unbowed by the condemnation, Miss Hazel made a triumphant ascension in San Jose, California, before boarding a train to perform at Sacramento in April 1891. As the balloon inflated for her second performance in the city's Oak Park, she escaped catastrophe when it exploded just moments before she mounted the trapeze bar. Following two hours spent sewing the tear, America's aerial thrill artist sailed again, to the delight of an "immense throng." Miss Hazel and Prof. Romig then executed a series of double parachute jumps at Oakland's Laundry Farm Resort in June 1891, where gigantic crowds flooded the grounds. Outfitted with a marvelous new balloon straight from the factory, Miss Hazel earned a reported $300 ($9,359 in 2021) for each ascension and parachute jump she completed. The couple used vapor of alcohol and gasoline to inflate the bag, dubbed "one of the largest ever seen on this Coast."[28]

Excitement peaked on June 29 before "one of the most extraordinary and thrilling spectacles ever witnessed on this side of the continent." This skydive unraveled in a flash, however. While warming up with exercises on a swing, sunstroke hit Miss Hazel, forcing postponement of her ascension and requiring Dr. Thomas' care to help her regain consciousness. Then, before Prof. Romig had arranged himself under the balloon, a malicious voice in the crowd yelled, "Let her go." The four men holding down the bag released their grip, and it shot into the sky. Romig jumped to catch his parachute and kept a precarious hold on it as the balloon climbed. "Nearly overcome with fright," Miss Hazel stared skyward to see her man dangling from the balloon. Clutching the rope that secured his chute to the bag, the Prof. climbed about one mile before his parachute caught air, and he floated to ground. The pair arranged to perform a double parachute jump for free in the future.[29]

Miss Hazel would perform on the balloon/parachute-jump circuit over the next 11 years, painting a legend of determination and courage across the heavens and the turf. Her story provides a glimpse into the traveling performer's life on the hard edge of the late-19th century and one of the nation's most remarkable parachuting careers. In an arena where few walked away, the spirited woman always wore a small golden cross, studded with precious stones, that a priest had given her to stave off bad luck when parachuting. Compromised by concussions, throttled for her cash by violent criminals, and brutalized by strangers, friends, loved ones, the law, and the earth itself, Miss Hazel Keyes survived a harried, thrill-filled existence on America's western frontier.

Sublime Summertime Pleasures Abound at Laundry Farm

"Situated in the most romantic section of the mountains overlooking Oakland and the bay," the Laundry Farm Hotel resort opened in 1892. "It is elevated so as to be beyond the reach of all fog, affording views of wide extent and unsurpassed beauty." A band played Sundays, and management sold no liquor at the family-oriented establishment. "The best class of people only are admitted," contended Traffic Manager W.M. Ranz. The facility's unique name stemmed from the 1850s when three San Francisco businessmen opened a laundry business at the site. Though the laundry enterprise moved to West Oakland in the 1860s, the area retained its Laundry Farm Canyon name. (*The Morning Call*, [San Francisco], June 14, 1891, "Laundry Farm"; inquisitivequest.com, Laundry Farm Canyon-Revealed #7; Alameda County, Illustrated; The Eden of the Pacific, The Flower Garden of California, Oakland, CA: Oakland Tribune Publishing, Co., 1898)

6

Sticky Fingers & Hard Knock Reality

While she dazzled the multitudes with her skyrobatic escapades at Oakland's Laundry Farm Resort, Miss Hazel's husband, Joseph Keyes, worked at a San Francisco butcher shop. Not long on the job, Joseph began pilfering money from his employer's cash drawer. Owner John T. Markell soon noticed that "a large falling off in his receipts" coincided with Keyes' employment and hired Detective James Rogers to confirm his suspicions.

Miss Hazel Keyes
America's Parachuting Queen
Akron Daily Democrat [Ohio], June 24, 1893

The savvy sleuth passed marked coins to customers who purchased their meat with them. Rogers found that "none of the coins reached the till" and "Keyes had been using his pocket instead of his employer's money drawer." Arrested at the butcher shop, Joseph folded in a flash, confessing and returning $100 to the meat man. Police later searched his clothes at the station, found several more marked coins, and charged him with two counts of petty larceny.

The theft case soon filled with the drama that often colored Miss Hazel Keyes' sensational saga. Her ankles aching from an earlier parachute jump, Miss Hazel visited San Francisco's City Prison in Old City Hall a few hours after her husband's incarceration. She arrived in a horse-drawn hospital gurney "neatly dressed" and hobbled up to the prison gate to ask for Joseph. Initially unrecognized, when she removed her veil "under the gaslight, she was identified as Hazel Keyes, the aeronaut," explained a news report. Bystanders witnessed Miss Hazel's fury over her husband's arrest.[30]

ROBBED HIS EMPLOYER.

Hazel Keyes' Husband Caught by Means of Marked Coin.

John T. Markell, a butcher doing business at 1413 Stockton street, noticed of late that there was a large falling off in his receipts. He puzzled over the matter to account for the shortage, and then it dawned on him that the decrease had become very noticeable after the employment of Joseph Keyes as clerk.

To settle the question, Markell enlisted the services of Detective Rogers. The detective had a lot of coin marked and passed by custom-

San Francisco Examiner, June 10, 1891

The case exposed police court shenanigans when it finally came to trial. Joseph vanished after his attorneys posted a $400 bond, forcing them to request several continuances. Frustrated by the delays, Butcher Markell and Detective Rogers demanded the judge issue a bench warrant for Keyes' arrest. The court clerk then revealed that "some unknown person without authority" stamped "released on his own recognizance" on the court calendar. This action concealed the posted bond and allowed Joseph to disappear long before officials discovered the illegally doctored document. The judge declared, "It would be an unheard-of proceeding to release a man on his own recognizance when he had already given bonds. Someone interested in the case has been tampering with the records."

Shouting "Crookedness in Court," San Francisco's *Morning Call* stated, "It was rumored about the musty old City Hall yesterday that $325 was paid [to] certain men who engineered the crooked manipulation" to "have [the] court mutilated." An attentive observer might question the extent to which Miss Hazel played a role in the deception that freed her husband. Later, one court official stood "firmly convinced that the man who fell from his parachute recently in Illinois and was killed is the much sought-for prisoner." No discovered facts support the theory. However, beset with tragedy, jealous suspicion, theft, and temptation, Miss Hazel's marriage to Joseph A. Keyes dissolved after this time.[31]

Her ankles throbbing and her husband subverting the law, Miss Hazel's luck took a turn for the worse when she made a morning ascension at Martinez, California's 1891 Fourth of July celebration. A "pleasant, bright-eyed, capable-looking little personage of modest demeanor and methods of conversation," she rose smoothly. At about 600 feet, the balloon exploded! Miss Hazel jumped with her parachute but found the distance above the earth inadequate and slammed into the dirt. One scribe declared, "No serious danger is anticipated," despite the aeronaut reinjuring her ankle and severely bruising her elbow. True to journalistic norms of the day, the report ignored Miss Hazel's plight, focusing instead on Manager Romig, who "attribute[d] his ill-luck [her balloon bursting] to the strong wind blowing."[32]

Though Miss Hazel's ankle injuries would plague the balance of her parachuting days, the phrase "no serious danger anticipated [or damage or worries]" and its sister comment, "not seriously injured," provided an enduring theme in her flabbergasting career. Despite the dismissive phrases, reports often described bruises, lacerations, her unconscious state, and concussion-like symptoms following hard and misdirected landings.

Santa Monica Beach hosts jubilant crowds in this ca.1900 image. A row of buildings lines the boardwalk, and an American flag flutters from a flagpole. Legible signs include: "Bowling alley, shooting gallery," "Arcadia Bath House, clean, smooth, safe beach, "Arcadia Grill Room," "Milkshake, lemonade," and "Bicycle riding prohibited on walk." (USCL, CHS-820, https:// doi.org/10.25549/chs-m6659)

As August 1891 started, Miss Hazel and the Prof. executed Santa Monica, California's first double parachute jump. Frolickers flooded the beach on a delicious southern California afternoon as gaiety flourished. Douglas' Military Band thundered out one of its most rousing airs as the pair, dressed in "circus attire," soared into the sky beneath a single balloon. Returning to earth, both parachutists landed with grace, stirring the hearts of spectators who witnessed the city's historic event.

The treachery of their profession always just a click away; trouble stalked Miss Hazel and Prof. Romig when they returned to Santa Monica later that August. Just before the duo's planned balloon race, a can of naphtha, used for igniting a fire beneath the balloon to fill it with heated air, exploded. Prof. Romig suffered burns to his face and hands, but ever the showman and not anxious to lose the day's receipts; he performed despite his injuries. When he and Miss Hazel ascended, thousands thrilled as their colorful balloons sailed past the city's Arcadia Hotel. Scaling the heights, they disappeared until Romig dove from his balloon, his parachute opened, and he eased downward.[33]

When Miss Hazel cut loose from her balloon, her parachute wobbled erratically. "Spectators watched [her] thrilling descent with bated breath," explained a *Los Angeles Herald* reporter. "Miss Keyes was tossed

Coastal climate inspired one scribe to muse, "The delightful weather makes the days glide by long before the pleasure-seekers are ready. The unrivaled evenings with their many enjoyments are far too short for the belles and beaux." (Los Angeles Herald, *August 1, 1891, "Santa Monica."*)

from side to side, but she clung to the trapeze [bar]. When she reached *terra firma*, a sigh of relief went up from the multitude." The sky-swirler affirmed, "I am all right. The wind was very strong and was responsible for the parachute turning so much. It was the most thrilling jump I ever made. I never had a parachute act like the one this afternoon." In September 1891, one journalist observed, "There is death in the parachute. Of late, the newspapers have recorded a loss of life from this cause out of all proportion to the practical value of the parachute, which is no value at all." Undeterred by disaster's imminence, Miss

Edwin Meeker completed this gorgeous illustration of the California Capitol at Sacramento in 1888. Constructed between 1860 and 1874, the building joined the National Register of Historical Places in 1973. (https://upload.wikimedia.org/wikipedia/commons/e/ed/The_Capitol%2C_Sacramento_-_EJM._LCCN2014645223.jp)

Hazel boarded a Sacramento-bound train for a California State Fair sky extravaganza.[34]

Perhaps due to Prof. Romig's burns suffered in the naphtha accident at Santa Monica, Miss Hazel faced off at Sacramento with aeronaut Professor F.J. Awerkamp in a balloon and parachute race. One bright September Saturday afternoon, a good-sized crowd settled in and around Agricultural Park to watch the race. A bell rang three times following the day's horse races to signal the balloon race's start, and the aerialists vaulted aloft. Both hovered at about 1,500 feet, where Prof. Awerkamp performed "daring gyrations" before each contestant dropped a handkerchief, signaling readiness.

When the bell clanged again, they leaped toward the crowd. Heavier than Miss Hazel, Prof. Awerkamp landed two seconds before her to claim a $100 prize. The *Sacramento Daily Record-Union* declared the city "fortunate in having two such accomplished aeronauts here. They are both experts, and to see either of them make an ascension and parachute jump is worth traveling many miles to witness. A balloon race is a novelty rarely witnessed."[35]

PROFESSOR AWERKAMP.

Sacramento Daily Record-Union,
August 18, 1890

After a group of San Joaquin Valley *vaqueros* failed to arrive for their "bronco-breakers" exhibition, Miss Hazel performed in pink tights and a blue blouse. Described as an "undaunted young spinster of pleasing facial appearance and athletic build," she settled to earth near Nineteenth Street and the city's north levee. Her descent sent icy chills through several women in carriages nearby. One complained, "It's all very well, but just suppose she had landed on [a] horse; what would have become of the poor animal?"[36]

Landing without incident, Miss Hazel continued to suffer ankle pain but deemed the latest leap one of her "most successful." Admittedly "pretty light" for her giant balloon, she agreed that her parachute did "sometimes sway violently." An observer declared that the parachute lurched so much she could "look horizontally through the opening in the top, but it always righted itself. Notwithstanding the lady's confidence in her parachute, it would seem that there is danger of its collapsing. Several times, it turned almost on its side, and it would seem that a sudden gust of wind might sometime overturn it." Nevertheless, Keyes explained that she feared no "danger of her parachute collapsing or being overturned."[37]

Miss Hazel next traveled to Los Angeles' Westlake (MacArthur) Park for several October 1891 engagements. The smell of 5-cent Red

Clover cigars and fresh-puffed popcorn hung over a boisterous crowd of 10,000 as she prepared to take a small monkey, Miss Jennie Yan Yan, into the sky. "I had constructed Yan Yan's parachute myself and was uncertain of its stability and consequently very nervous about cutting her loose," the aerialist later explained. "If anything went wrong and the animal was killed, I should have suffered not alone, the loss of my pet, but the adverse comment of the press and the public. It would, perhaps, have resulted in my having to abandon a field in which I was popular and successful." However, she added, "Anyone engaged in so risky a business as mine has but little time or use for nervous apprehensions; or [they] could not follow it under the strain of a constant fear."[38]

Miss Hazel Keyes' October 1891 performance at Los Angeles' Westlake Park ended with her crashing to earth and suffering cognitive consequences. The city renamed the grounds MacArthur Park to honor General Douglas MacArthur in 1942. A horse-drawn buggy rolls through in this period image. (University of Southern California Libraries, [USCL], California Historical Society [CHS]-5058, https://doi.org/10.25549/chs-m3724) https://doi.org/10.25549/chs-m3724)

While her monkey suffered no reported ill effects, Miss Hazel fared far worse. Her balloon surged to about 1,200 feet, where she fought an intense wind after her parachute opened. She sawed her feet back and forth in frantic effort to control the erratic, zig-zagging chute—to no avail. Dropping in a flash, she landed on her side about 300 feet from the end of a nearby cable car line. Transported to her hotel, physicians soon revived her. The physicians' statement read, "Not seriously injured," and declared, "She fainted away." Here, one might speculate regarding the enduring toll of pain, such collisions with the earth exact, and their cumulative debt. Biological and anatomical science suggest that their sum might create a usurious tax upon one corporeal vessel. Yet, flashy in her colorful tights, America's durable Parachute Queen pressed ahead with Thanksgiving and Christmas ascensions at Adolph Gasson's Pacific Beach Driving Park near San Diego.[39]

Animals in the Air! Entertaining Animals: Righteous or Wrong?

The use of animals for entertainment appears to have originated around 2,000 B.C. with the caging of lions in Macedonia. Popularized by Circus Maximus in ancient Rome with chariot racing and gladiator/lion battles, animal entertainment thrived during the 1890s. Oft referred to as the "Golden Age of the Circus," the decade featured small traveling "wagon circuses" and industry behemoths Barnum & Bailey and Ringling Brothers. The widespread popularity of animal performances and their repulsiveness to many springs from the same well—anthropomorphism—attributing human traits and emotions to non-human creatures.

Journalistic references to anthropomorphism reached a modern statistical apex in the 1890s. On one pillar stood those who couldn't help but giggle, guffaw, or gawk in awe at the absurdity and irony of a monkey parachuting or collecting change for its organ-grinder or dancing bears in pink tutus. Their counterforce condemned the obligatory compliance of performing animals to their human masters. Contemplating such a terrifying, demeaning, dangerous oppression of animal rights fueled societal anger. As primates, monkeys in particular fired the paying public's passions.

French papermakers Jacques-Étienne and Joseph-Michael Montgolfier launched a sheep Montauciel (Mount-the-Sky), a duck, and a rooster as the first living creatures to leave the earth on September 19, 1783.

Mr. Clayton first sent a dog in a parachute off a Court Street theater roof in Cincinnati, Ohio, in April 1835. Its owner, Mr. Hazen, eschewed a $100 payment because he felt the canine would "be sufficiently popular to run for Vice President" after it flew. When it sailed, a young fellow named Hose caught the pup before it landed and declared for posterity, "Gentlemen and Ladies! This the dog wot come down in the Parachute! He's as sound as when he was put in! He lit near the canal, and I'm the chap wot cotched him. He's as good as when he left here with Mr. Clayton! He's not stunned! Nor scared!! Nor hurt!!! Nor nothing!!!!"

Mrs. Murphy, a trained monkey, "prayed" before takeoff and then parachuted 1,000 feet by herself from a balloon. The animal toured Europe, making 150 parachute jumps before performing in the United States about 1899. West Virginia's *Clarksburg Telegram* declared the monkey "appears to show almost human intelligence." (*The Clarksburg Telegram,* [West Virginia], August 31, 1900, "This Monkey Plays Aeronaut"; *Richmond Palladium,* [Indiana], April 18, 1835, "Balloon Ascension.")

7

Monkey on High, "Nice Catch!" & A Torturous Ride

A star in her own right, Miss Jennie Yan Yan's history shone! A *San Francisco Examiner* reporter explained that a sailor captured the monkey "in a Kongo [sic] coconut tree" and sold her to a San Francisco waterfront peddler. When Miss Hazel saw the "serious-faced monkey and her impressive countenance," she purchased her parachuting partner, and the pair "soon became friends." Claiming the animal "never trembled" while in the air, the account explained, "The intelligent simian soon learned to detach the ropes [of her parachute] and descend." The monkey's fame grew as "many thousands along the [west] coast" watched her remarkable aerial exhibitions. One day, Miss Jennie managed to untie the "slender fastenings" that secured her to a cage and head for the city sidewalk. An Italian gentleman with "bright visions of organ-grinding victories" grabbed "the chance of a lifetime" and scooped up the wandering monkey. Searching in frantic angst for her beloved companion, Miss Hazel met a street laborer who witnessed Yan Yan's abduction. Feisty and furious, Miss Hazel snatched her chattering and grinning monkey back from the would-be-organ-grinder and secured it with a heavy chain and padlock to "avert the possibility of a permanent loss."[40]

Miss Jennie made a series of parachute descents with Miss Hazel at Los Angeles in mid-February 1892. The aeronaut "laughingly" explained that, though her pet "never said much about it," the animal had grown to "thoroughly" enjoy parachuting. Keyes declared: "She is very jealous of her parachute and will permit no one but us to touch it. [She] will sharply assault anyone who tries to touch it or her after she has reached *terra firma*." While the sky-plunging combo prepared for their show, agitated spectators summoned Humane Society Officer Wright, but he arrived after the pair had ascended. All went well as the two balloons flew away, and after Miss Hazel cut the rope to set her trained simian sailer free, the animal landed safely about 100 feet from her. A *Los Angeles Herald* journalist stated, "Many people have perhaps supposed that Humane Officer Wright was derelict in not preventing Miss Hazel Keyes from dropping her monkey."[41]

Both performers back on earth, the officer demanded that Miss Hazel allow him to examine the monkey for injuries. Readily agreeing, right after she changed her clothes, she swept up Miss Jennie and carried her into the dressing room of a nearby store. When Miss Hazel failed to reappear and Officer Wright refused to abandon his duty, the shop owner hailed a police officer, who ordered Wright to leave. The *Herald* scribe declared, "The law, prohibiting cruelty to animals, it appears, does not cover the case unless the monkey suffered physical harm. It [the law] takes no cognizance of cruelty when it takes the form of terrorizing helpless creatures." Several reports, however, told of Miss Jennie Yan Yan exhibiting a fervent desire to ride the skies with her partner and demonstrating extreme distress when barred from doing so.[42]

Prof. J.J. Romig rejoined Miss Hazel and Miss Jennie Yan Yan in Sacramento on spring 1892's first day. Thousands paid 10 cents admission to relish the intrepid performers' dance among the clouds at Agricultural Park. Matters did not progress as planned, however. With an aroused horde pressing closer to the balloon each moment, Miss

Frenchman Henri Lachambre (1846–1904) employed this fanciful image of balloons floating among real and imaginary creatures to promote his balloon-making business. Lachambre reported 500 balloon ascensions and provided the balloon for S.A. Andrée's star-crossed 1897 attempt to reach the North Pole by hydrogen balloon. He also worked with noted Brazilian aviation pioneer Alberto Santos-Dumont. (Library of Congress—LC-DIG-ppmsca-02488)

DROPPING FROM THE CLOUDS.

GRAND BALLOON ASCENSION AND
Double Parachute Drop at Agricultural
Park by MISS HAZEL KEYES and the
monkey Yan Yan, SUNDAY, March 20th, at
3 P. M. sharp; one balloon and two parachutes,
the monkey will come down in his own
monkey parachute. General admission, 10c.1*

Sacramento Record-Union, March 19, 1891

Hazel's assistants removed the upright posts that secured it. She held tight to her trapeze bar hanging beneath the bag, and with "Let go," it vaulted toward the heavens. At its release, a strong northwest wind shoved the balloon into a pulley block atop one of the support posts.

Miss Hazel's trapeze bar caught on the post with a violent jerk, snapping the rope connecting her to the balloon and plunging her about 30 feet to the ground. Men swooped her up and rushed her, unconscious, to a room beneath the grandstand. Prof. Romig explained,

"She is not hurt seriously. The accident was caused by the crowd being unmanageable and pressing in so closely that we could not remove the supports in time. We couldn't keep the crowd back." A doctor arrived in short order to report Miss Hazel "not dangerously hurt," with "no bones broken." In truth, pain stabbed the flyer in her side, and she remained unconscious. Speaking "incoherently until removed in a cab," she yelled "repeatedly to her attendants to 'Let go the rope!' and 'Don't let it go, Tom, don't!'" Battered but unbeaten, Miss Hazel revived her career two months later with a parachute leap at Portland, Oregon's Blue House Park. She next enjoyed her most miraculous and dramatic rescue from crash-landing.[43]

Bears, kangaroos, sea lions, and other animals delighted spectators who swarmed Seattle's Leschi Park along Lake Washington's western shore. Boats lolled on the glistening water, and the Langer & Lueben's Band tuned up for their concert as Miss Hazel and Miss Jennie prepared to parachute above Seattle on May 22, 1892. Revelers covered the park's casino terraces, climbing the trestles and filling the surrounding hillsides. All eyes fixed upon Miss Hazel as she left the ground's west side. When she cut free of the balloon, her parachute failed to open cleanly and slow her descent. She plummeted toward the earth, and her demise appeared certain. In a sudden flash, fate's fortuitous hero dashed into peril's devilish gap—Officer Stepler! The day's champion reached out to miraculously clutch its crashing star, gently but decisively cushioning Miss Hazel's landing. Improbably, neither catcher nor catchee reported injury. Such a fantastic feat fairly laughs in the face of reality, yet observers affirmed the account! Meanwhile, Miss Jennie Yan Yan landed unharmed in Lake Washington near the shore. Plans called for the monkey, a sopping ball of fur, to reside at the city zoo during Miss Hazel's remaining northwest exhibitions.[44]

Encounters with the unmovable created stiff problems in the parachuting world. Miss Hazel's August 14, 1892 act at Seattle's Madison Street Park sliced a sharp tip on that point. That day, she and Prof. Romig boarded separate balloons in a vacant lot south of the park's ball fields. As they started, winds pushed them straight toward Lake Washington and a picket fence surrounding the fields. Romig realized he would slam into the fence and performed a running jump. The balloon gave him a swift jerk, and he cleared it but hit a spectator under the chin, knocking him out.

Miss Hazel fared far worse.

DRAGGED ON A FENCE.

Hazel Keyes, the Aeronaut, Terribly Injured.

HER NERVE AND COOLNESS.

The Balloon, Slow to Ascend, Drags Her Over the Fence—Her Injuries May Prove Fatal.

While making the balloon ascension and parachute jump at Madison street park yesterday afternoon Hazel Keyes, the lady

Seattle Post-Intelligencer, August 15, 1892

Leading with her diaphragm, the diminutive mademoiselle smashed into the fence's sharp points. Lakeshore winds then propelled her along its top in a torturous ride. "So quickly did the whole affair take place that only a few persons noticed that she was injured," stated an observer. "With wonderful nerve, she hung to the balloon and when it was over the lake, cut loose and sailed gently downward." The stricken woman hit the water just northeast of the lake's wharf, where the crew of a waiting boat hoisted her unconscious form from the bay. Revived, Miss Hazel told the men of her injuries, and they took her into a room at Seattle's Madison Street powerhouse to await Dr. W.M. Hilton. *The Seattle Post-Intelligencer* reported that before his arrival, she succumbed to "an epileptic fit, frothed at the mouth, talked incoherently, and became insensible." When Dr. Hilton arrived, he found Miss Hazel's left ankle sprained and "the toes of the foot crushed painfully." The physician explained, "The most dangerous injury was in the body just below the chest. The exact effect the internal injuries will have cannot be told." Late night found the patient calm under opiate sedation and her doctor "in hopes that she would escape serious results," but warning that her injuries might "prove fatal."[45]

Less than two weeks after her accident, Miss Hazel initiated another astounding bounce-back from injury when she made ascensions at California's Napa Valley Fair. However, her aerial journey six weeks later at the San Mateo & Santa Clara County Fair in San Jose only enriched her pain. At 2,000 feet, she began a hair-raising descent in a fierce wind, and her parachute swung wildly from side to side like a colossal plumb bob. About to tip entirely over several times, Miss Hazel hung from her trapeze bar and landed on her feet before slamming onto her right side. People rushed to her aid and, finding her again unconscious, took her to her room in the city's California Block. Dr. Guyton's examination showed her ankles brutally sprained once again, her right arm bruised, an ugly cut behind her right ear, and her face badly scratched.[46]

Fashionably-attired revelers enjoy Seattle's Leschi Park in this period image. An important steamboat stop from 1890 to 1901, the park sat on Lake Washington at the end of the cable car line. (https://leschi-park-seattle-curtis-734-dc6efb)

8

Tragedy Sparks Sisterly Care & A Sweet Sausalito Swing

Tragedy brought Miss Hazel's kind heart to the fore in 1893. Circulating from fairgrounds to amusement parks throughout the nation on the parachuting performance circuit left little room for building enduring friendships. Miss Hazel thus thrilled to the companionship of 20-year-old Lillian "Lillie" Dean. Orphaned at just 10, the former waitress in a downtown San Francisco restaurant showed spunk and daring, hidden beneath a quiet and retiring veneer, endearing her to Miss Hazel. When Miss Hazel's balloon and parachute instructor, Professor Frank P. Hagal, met the young woman, he declared her "the nerviest girl I ever saw, and I've been a professional aeronaut for 20 years." Hagal soon agreed to employ Miss Lillie to parachute with him near the city's Cliff House. Though reportedly wed, Hagal declared their marriage "merely an advertising dodge."[47]

A fierce wind whipped off the Pacific Ocean on April 16, 1893, assaulting the beach north of the Cliff House. Scheduled to ascend and execute a parachute jump, Prof. Hagal instead sent Miss Lillie aloft into the ferocious gale. With the furnace beneath it thundering to build hot air, her balloon began to fill. Powerful gusts threatened to tear the guy ropes from the hands of 20 to 30 strong but inexperienced men who battled to contain it. A thousand spectators gathered as Miss Lillie fastened the hoop of the parachute around her left wrist. Dressed in flashy blue cotton tights, she stood ready to make only her fourth ascension. She carried circulars advertising a patented drink in her right arm to throw into the air when she cut loose from the balloon.

With raging gusts thrashing the balloon, her husband shouted, "Hold her; she's not full yet." However, a smart aleck in the crowd yelled, "All ready, let go." Prof. Hagal screamed, "For God's sake, men hold it! For God's sake, don't leave go!" But about six men on the windward side released their grip on the vast balloon. It bolted into the sky, throwing the other holders "in all directions like so many sticks of wood." Knocking several bricks loose from the furnace built to fill it with hot air, the balloon burst into flames and swept Miss Lillie across

LILLIE HAGAL.

Miss Lillie Dean

San Jose Evening News, April 17, 1893

the ground before ascending to about 40 feet. "As it rose burning, the gaping crowd at first seemed amused at the woman's endeavors to free herself," explained a *San Jose Evening News* story. "Their amusement speedily changed to anxiety, then to horror as they saw the balloon rise. An involuntary 'Oh!' came from the horror-stricken assemblage."

A two-story wooden frame saloon and dance hall and a fifteen-foot-tall shanty housing a tintype gallery stood on a cliff above the beach about 200 yards away. Dragging her by the wrist, the burning balloon slammed

Miss Lillie into the saloon's second story, shattering a window. She flew across the building's roof, shredding shingles as she went. Over the railroad tracks running from the Cliff House to the bayside ferries, her helpless body sailed, smashing into the eaves of the tintype gallery's roof and shattering both of her femurs. The fierce wind broke the balloon free, and it fell to a charred demise. Miss Lillie's unconscious form hung about 12 feet above the ground with her left wrist pinned between two broken shingles. Nearby, women fainted, and men looked away in horror as fellow aeronaut J.H. Whiteside and others rushed to the scene with a ladder and carried her 106-pound body to safety.[48]

With her nose split and a ragged piece of bone poking out of her left thigh, the young woman survived her ordeal to lie in Ward G of San Francisco's Receiving Hospital. "Plastered and bandaged" so that she only could move her head, Miss Lillie suffered gut-wrenching agony as surgeons repaired her fractured bones. The pluck Miss Hazel admired endured, however. Miss Lillie vowed, "I'll go up again just as soon as I am able to walk." Physicians expressed confidence that "she may recover, as she shows remarkable vitality." However, the young woman succumbed to her injuries.

The death of her fellow aeronaut and Prof. Hagal's apparent lack of funds prompted Miss Hazel to collect enough money for a "suitable funeral for the poor girl who lost her life at the beginning of a perilous career,"

A San Francisco Chronicle *artist reflected Miss Lillie Dean's tragic end.* (San Francisco Chronicle, *April 17, 1893)*

noted a *San Francisco Chronicle* correspondent. "By these means, Lillie Dean, a stranger in this city, was saved from a pauper's grave." Bereft, Miss Hazel stood alongside a dozen mourners attending Miss Lillie's ceremony at a Geary Street undertaking house. Two floral pieces and several bouquets marked her grave in the inexpensive Tier 16 of San Francisco's Laurel Hill Cemetery's Cosmopolitan Plat.[49]

In an odd twist, grave robbers soon violated the sanctity of Miss Lillie's burial site. Grieving her death the day after the funeral, Prof. Hagal jumped the cemetery's fence and headed for Miss Lillie's grave. As he approached, he spotted two scoundrels in their lantern's dim light. The pair hurried off into the darkness, and he saw the horror. The men had dug down to her casket, destroyed it, and made off with Miss Lillie's corpse. Believing he caught the body snatchers ready to fill the grave back in with dirt, Hagal rushed to the local police station. Speculation ran to the "ghouls' (real professionals)" hopes of selling the bones to a medical college as the motive. A recent burial might have also meant easier digging in freshly packed soil, and the disturbed soil would have appeared natural at a recent burial site.[50]

Double Danger

Tragically, Professor Hagal's next bride also died in a parachuting accident just two years after Miss Lillie Dean. Miss Nellie Hagal placed an unsuccessful Help Wanted ad for a "Lady to learn to be an aeronaut and go on the stage" in July 1895. That September, she slammed to earth on her back from 1,000 feet when her left hand slipped from her safety rope at Monrovia, California. (*Los Angeles Times*, July 27, 1895, "Help Wanted—Female"; *San Francisco Chronicle*, September 30, 1895, "Slipped from a Parachute.")

The year 1893 brought a perfect storm of economic pain to the nation. Like so many toothpicks, pillars of the financial system crashed. That February, Philadelphia & Reading Railroad defaulted, and in April, the U.S. Treasury's Gold Reserve fell below its $100-million minimum. Fears of the federal government's ability to exchange dollars for gold coins, specie, fired a "run" on banks. The ensuing Panic of 1893 crushed stock markets and forced the closure of 575 banks and 15,000 businesses. Unemployment more than tripled, sending many people to local soup kitchens. Reports of Miss Hazel's parachuting escapades might have brightened more than a few dreary outlooks that summer, if ever so briefly. She boasted more than 150 hot-air ascents when workers hoisted her balloon's guy-wires from their mooring pins at Sausalito, California's railroad wharf, on June 4, 1893. Prof. Romig had worked his way along the Sausalito waterfront, soliciting money from saloon keepers and businessmen to raise $75 and fund the performance.[51]

Resplendent "in all the glory of purple fleshings" and intent on parachuting onto Kershaw Island's Belvedere Heights, Miss Hazel rose with her monkey. Shooting "heavenward like a startled eagle," the colorful balloon whipped about before catching a stiff wind. The pair sailed east over Richardson Bay toward Angel Island, affording them stunning views of San Francisco and beyond. Her balloon lost air, however, and Miss Hazel sailed toward the rigging of the schooner U.S.S. *J.B. Walker* about a half-mile offshore. Terrified screams rang out, "They are going to strike the ship! They'll surely be killed!" Then commenced "a scene as exciting as any ever seen in the bay off Sausalito."[52]

Heading straight toward the ship's foremast, Miss Hazel employed her exceptional athleticism to execute a remarkable, life-saving maneuver. Dodging the sturdy wooden foremast and a dastardly death, she swung around it and threw her right leg over the end of the fore-topgallant yardarm. Almost turning a complete somersault in the air, the daring aeronaut hung upside-down with her other leg trapped in the rigging's ropes. At the same time, she yanked the string, which freed her from the parachute before it could drag her into the water. She remained adangle, cursing until a crew member scurried up the rigging and helped her sit upright on the yardarm. Thunderous cheers erupted from an anxious crowd onshore.[53]

Miss Jennie Yan Yan's pathetic plight earned sympathy. She first slammed against a mass of telegraph wires during the ascent. Then,

What Thrilled the Crowd.

A Morning Call *artist's illustration of Miss Hazel Keyes hanging in the ropes of the U.S.S. J.B. Walker.* (The Morning Call [San Francisco], June 5, 1893)

splashing into the bay, the propeller of the steam launch *Mary McNeil* snagged the ropes of her parachute as it raced to rescue her. Pulled free of the tangle, the sopping monkey inspired Bay Area journalists to charge Miss Hazel with animal abuse. In San Francisco, *The Morning Call* scribe decried "the pitiful bowing and grimaces of the elderly lady in tights."[54]

A *San Francisco Examiner* writer issued a searing condemnation of Miss Hazel. Recounting the thousands who swarmed the Sausalito waterfront and hills to view "an act of revolting cruelty," the columnist declared, "The shivering, crying little fellow [monkey] was all but dead." A *Sausalito News* reporter also focused on the woes and tribulations of Miss Hazel's furry partner. The writer deduced a fantastical array of monkey-specific communications by the "uncultivated little creature from the coast of Africa." The animal felt "indignant and vindictive" and launched a tantrum necessitating "the presence of Constable Creed to pacify her nerves and sweeten her temper," said the scribe. "The moment she saw his glittering star, she became as quiet and submissive as a city hoodlum in his hands."[55]

Demonstrating further faith in interspecies communication, the monkey-sympathetic reporter tore into the teeth of reality:

"In the presence of her mistress, Yan Yan sat in Creed's lap and related the pathetic effect of the cruel wrongs inflicted upon her by Miss Keyes, whose only ambition was money and notoriety. When the poor thing alluded to its parents in the Far East and the streams upon which she strayed in childhood, every cheek was made wet with tears, the writer weeping aloud."[56]

Miss Hazel's marvelous escape from doom brought her national renown as the news raced through Kansas, Ohio, and further east to New York, Maryland, and Delaware. Captain McKenzie of the ferry steamer San Rafael witnessed the phenomenal move and stated, "That was the greatest aerial feat I ever saw in my life. That woman flew through the air like a seagull." Unfazed as usual, Miss Hazel insisted, "I've made over 150 hot-air balloon ascensions, and I hope to make many more. Today was the most successful of all. I must have reached 3,000 feet," and "the residences of Sausalito looked like chicken coops. Suddenly, the balloon began to weaken and descend. I wanted to save the monkey above all things." She added, "Of course, I shall make another ascension at the first opportunity, as it is my profession and the way I make my living. It is very dangerous, I know, for had I struck the mast or yard of the ship, I was liable to be killed."[57]

Launched in 1879 as an American Seagoing Barge, the schooner U.S.S. J.B. Walker later served the U.S. Navy during World War I. (U.S. Naval Historical Center NH 102504)

9

Animal Cruelty Seeks Definition in Seattle Showdown

M iss Hazel returned to Seattle's Madison Street Park one year after her horrible, near-deadly picket fence accident. One Sunday in July 1893, found Miss Jennie Yan Yan in a lather when Seattle Humane Society Detective John Roberts tried to bar her from ascending. Miss Hazel battled the man with her distinctive ferocity, demanding to see his "papers giving him authority." She later reported that Roberts "replied in an impudent manner that he did not have to show them or his badge." Miss Hazel acknowledged hearing Roberts say that she should not take the monkey airborne but declared in defiance that she had "heard people talk like that before."[58]

Apprised of the ruckus, a raucous crowd encircled the combatants. The monkey's parachute lay on the ground while the animal remained tethered to Miss Hazel's wrist with a string. Thrills peaked as she mounted her balloon and announced, "All ready!" In that instant, Detective Roberts grabbed for Miss Jennie. "Let go that monkey," shouted the indignant skydiver. "All was confusion," chuckled a reporter. "Roberts clung on; the monkey clawed; the crowd laughed." Not one to watch his wife abused by an overzealous copper, Prof. J.J. Romig rushed in to hop the fight, and as he rolled in the dirt clutching Roberts, Miss Hazel's balloon sailed into the sky, sans monkey.

BALLOON ASCENSION!

MADISON PARK.

Sunday Afternoon, July 16, at 3 O'clock

MISS HAZEL KEYES,

Queen

OF ALL

Aerialists

Seattle Post-Intelligencer, July 15, 1893

An unknown person cut her string leash, and Miss Jennie Yan Yan bounded around in wild convulsions. As the balloon flew away, she lost sight of her aeronautic partner and grew more befuddled. Jumping aboard street railway car No. 6, the crazed primate frightened several women before leaping out and sprinting around between the streetcars. When she saw her owner's balloon, she raced along beneath it. Stopping atop the roof of the Laurel Shade at Patrick Scullin's summer garden, Miss Jennie began prattling and making "symbolic gestures" as Miss Hazel splashed into Lake Washington.[59]

Aground, Detective Roberts battled Miss Hazel to control the monkey and soon found himself in trouble with spectators who gathered around. "The detective found little sympathy among the crowd" and proved "the object of many uncomplimentary remarks. It is safe to say that Hazel Keyes thinks he is the most contemptible of men." Roberts arrested Miss Hazel on a charge of animal cruelty and hauled her downtown, still in her wet clothes. She declared: "It would have been her fiftieth ascension, and she has yet to be hurt a bit."[60]

Keyes stated that Roberts "got very nervous" when she said, "All ready," and grabbed Jennie Yan Yan. "It [was] really laughable to see him trying to get someone to cut the rope by which I held her and, for a moment, it was a tugging match. In fact, he came near pulling my finger off. I do not know who cut the string, but I went up without Jennie. While

FUN WITH A MONKEY.

Struggle to Prevent Her Ascending in a Balloon.

HAZEL KEYES RESISTS ROBERTS

He Rescues the Monkey and the Husband Shows Fight—Aeronaut and Husband Arrested.

Jennie Yan Yan, the monkey that is in the habit of making aerial ascensions with Hazel Keyes, the female aeronaut, did not

Seattle Post-Intelligencer, July 14, 1893

coming down, [I] saw her sitting on the roof at the Laurel Shade making signs to me." Twenty-five dollars freed Miss Hazel on bail, and her husband paid $50 for his freedom on a charge of interfering with an officer. Despite locking her up, Miss Hazel, Humane Society officials, the Madison Street Railway Company, and Detective Roberts held a courtroom "love feast" the following day.[61]

Rescuers plucked Miss Hazel Keyes from Seattle's Lake Washington's chilly waters near Madison Park. (Madison Park on Lake Washington, circa 1892.JPG)

10

How Flight Feels & "Despicable Footpads"

The Misses Hazel and Jennie Yan Yan visited Olympia, Washington's Old Fair Grounds following their Seattle struggles. Before Miss Hazel arrived at the fairgrounds, workers dug a 3-foot-square fire pit and a 20-foot-long covered trench leading to a flue about 6 feet tall over which they arranged the balloon. Igniting dry wood in the hole, Miss Hazel fed it frequent doses of gasoline, which built a roaring blaze. As the heated air traveled through the trench and up the flue, her canvas bag grew to 70 feet tall by 50 feet in diameter. After the balloon filled sufficiently, Miss Hazel settled onto her trapeze bar, and her "Let Go!" cry sent the device shooting upwards.[62]

Miss Jennie Yan Yan rode a three-foot parachute down before Miss Hazel cut the rope freeing her own chute. "The ascent was fearfully rapid and seemed to be equal to the speed of the famous Limited Express trains on the leading Eastern railroads—nearly a mile a minute," claimed a *Washington Standard* reporter. Both parachutes landed in Tumwater Bay, Miss Hazel just 10 feet from the shore near Crosby's Mill. Her speed, however, thrust her far below the surface. A person who saw her alight raced to meet her and told the laughing woman, "I thought you would never come up!"

Dry once again, the sky-sailing star explained her flying experience in detail. "Why, it is simply delightful," she began. "There is no indication of any other motion except the swaying of the ropes from side to side and from the rush of wind by your ears. After you have attained an elevation of 4,000 to 5,000 feet, the view is grand beyond the power of words to describe. You seem to float in a sea of ether, and your spirits are as light as those of the bird which goes twitting by, your only companion. The view is much different from that obtained, or the sensation experienced, on the mountain top. There you have spread out before you the many miles of incline."[63]

SOMETHING NEW
. . . IN THE . . .
Line of Amusement!
. . . AT THE . . .
OLD FAIR GROUNDS.
Sunday, August 20.
GRAND Balloon Ascension
AND DOUBLE PARACHUTE LEAP
By the Queen of all Aerialists,
MISS HAZEL KEYES
And the Famous Performing Monkey, Jennie Yan Yan.
The name of Miss Hazel Keyes assures success of the performance. She has made nearly 300 ascensions without a failure.

The Washington Standard, August 11, 1893

Capturing an outlook few, if any, of her admirers attained, Miss Hazel expounded, "The verdure of the trees beneath me, today, appeared as a great carpeting of moss. The bay seemed like a sheet of silver, bordered by deeper hues and the reflection of the distant mountains. The houses of your city appeared about the size of dry-goods boxes. The people directly underneath me grew into minute dots until finally, lost from view as identities and individuals, [they] could only be distinguished by a slightly different coloring from the grass and buildings."

Quizzed by an admirer if she had ever flown through clouds, the confident skydiver answered, "Yes, I have went [sic] through clouds, in making an ascent. The moisture is in the form of a mist instead of drops. It is during the descent of the rain that these particles unite and form drops. The sensation in passing through the clouds is like a vapor bath, only with several degrees of reduced temperature. When you are in the air, the surface of the earth presents a gradual rise in the distance all around you and assuming a concave appearance, instead of the real convexity which the rotundity of the earth affords."

Keyes continued, "The origin of my self-confidence, I presume, is in having had an experienced teacher [Frank P. Hagal]. I am now so familiar with all the varied experiences in mid-air that I am absolutely without fear. The only judgment I exercise is to select a good place to alight, and I cast off so as to fall somewhat near the place chosen. The parachute, in the hands of an experienced person, is remarkably easy to manage. If you want to go to one side, you simply pull down on that side and ease up on the other. This shifts the top of the parachute so that as it falls, the air shoves it along just as it does the sail of a boat in tacking. I could have managed to return to the Fair Grounds today, but I preferred to drop in the water. You saw how near I dropped to shore and how little swimming I had to do to reach land." The enthralled *Washington Standard* reporter stated that Miss Hazel possessed "an excellent education, a vivacious temperament, and splendid conversational powers. She anticipated no danger from her perilous vocation."[64]

Chas. H. Kabrich's bicycle parachuting stunts won him admirers in the East and Midwest throughout the 1890s. (http://hdl.loc.gov/loc.pnp/cph.3a25431)

Miss Hazel Keyes and Miss Jennie Yan Yan posed for this November 2, 1893 image taken by renowned Oregon photographers Anna L. Cronise and Howard D. Trover. (Oregon Historical Society #A-886)

Miss Hazel married her passion and her pain, James J. Romig, in Portland, Oregon, on September 6, 1893. Filled with more peaks and pits than might attend a mountain of marriages, she and Prof. Romig continued their rollercoaster love affair for almost 50 years. The liaison would not serve them entirely well, yet both seemed chained to the task of ensuring its hot-blooded furtherance. The Keyes/Romig/Yan Yan aerial show headed to Salem, Oregon's State Fair Grounds for a run of ascensions during the fall of 1893. By this time, Miss Hazel had survived 276 solo parachute jumps and 52 double leaps with Romig, while Miss Jennie owned 66 skydives. Numerous escapes from death and career-ending injury had built Miss Hazel a national reputation. Deeming her "the most daring aerialist in the world," one writer declared, "Her boasted immunity from death and accident is no fable. She yet lives and perhaps will be seen many more times." The "fortunate" aerialist explained, "My scrutiny of the ropes and appliances which govern my undertakings is so keen and exhaustive that I leave the earth, always with a positive conviction that nothing can happen. My manipulations in the air are always in accordance with the conditions as I find them." These include the direction and strength of the wind and "the density or rarity of the atmosphere," which "determine the height to which I shall go, the drift I must make, and the conditions of my landing."[65]

Keyes continued, "A parachute is much like a tractable team of horses well driven. You can guide it to almost any given spot and alight where you please." The journalist noted, "No expense is spared in reducing the chances of disaster to a minimum. The balloon, ropes, gearing, the knife that precipitates the thrilling parachute jump, the construction of the [heating] trench, the inflation of the balloon, and the hundred other little details involved are all special and never neglected. She is eminently practical and cool-headed. Her sharp and eager oversight of these details contributes largely to the success of her work." Miss Hazel added, "No one ever troubles or insults me. The public is in warmer sympathy with a woman than with a man. In all my contacts with the roughest of rough crowds, I have never had the slightest trouble or annoyance."[66]

On November 5, 1893, Miss Hazel performed a flight to 8,000 feet, as measured by a device she carried with her. A double parachute jump in Salem with Miss Jennie followed. Some 2,000 admission-free spectators witnessed the duo take the sky east of the fairground's Pavilion. A fog bank soon engulfed their balloon, and they went out of view for about 10 minutes. Cheers rang forth as they reappeared, hanging from their parachutes below the cloud, and sailed to safety. With the engagement off to a good start, things turned ugly in Oregon's Cherry City.

While her husband took charge of the balloon that evening, Miss Hazel changed her clothes and left the Pavilion building. Tugging her coat tight around her, the short, attractive, sturdy young woman stepped into the venue's dark parking lot. Rushing out of the chilly Willamette River night, a "low, stout, heavy-set, smooth-faced man" leaped upon her from behind. The "despicable footpad" (robber who travels on foot) had studied his prey with a precision befitting his evil soul. Saying, "I have just been laying for you!" the crook snatched her by the dress and coat collar and hurled her backward to the ground, ripping her clothes. Searching through her coat pockets, the creep grabbed her money purse and departed with $46.76 ($1,575 in 2021). Miss Hazel screamed for help, but none arrived in time. She saw a man

Fair Grounds!

Grand Balloon Ascension and Double Parachute Jump

BY THE MOST DARING LADY AERIALIST IN THE WORLD,

Miss Hazel Keyes,

Who will astonish all beholders by her marvelous and graceful parachute descent from the clouds to the earth. Also the world-renowned performing monkey,

JENNIE YAN YAN.

—— DIRECT CARS ON BOTH LINES OF STREET RAILWAY. ——

THURSDAY

NOV.

2d

At 3:00 Sharp

THE WORLD RENOWNED MONKEY,

Jennie Yan Yan

Will ascend at the same time, and come down in her own monkey parachute.

Admission,   FREE!
NO HAT PASSED.

Oregon Daily Statesman (Salem),
November 1, 1893

standing about 100 feet from her and yelled, "Catch the thief," but the stealthy figure, seemingly an accomplice, streaked away into the night.[67]

Prof. Romig raced toward his wife but failed to catch the brigands, and a rush of men started after the crooks to no avail. Miss Hazel took the three-mile carriage ride into downtown Salem and arrived about eight o'clock that night. Reports said, "She was considerably excited and showed signs of having been pretty roughly handled but showed great pluck under the circumstances."[68]

Back in the sky, just four days later, Miss Hazel climbed to 2,200 feet before executing a smooth parachute landing. Her balloon, however, came down on a man's apple tree, breaking off a small branch. The "vexed owner" grabbed up the wayward balloon, hid it in his chicken coop, and demanded $25 in restitution from Miss Hazel, unaware of her nature and disposition. The *Weekly Oregon Statesman* writer picked up the tale and reported, "Miss Keyes at once went to the rescue of her aerial 'chum,'" which she retrieved "without delay and without price. The tree's owner wisely concluded, perhaps, that a woman of Miss Keyes' nerve and courage would resent very warmly such injustice."[69]

Foul fortune continued to stalk America's sky-jumping darling when a lapse in vigilance extracted another $105 from her pocketbook in early January 1894. Standing at the window of her room in Sacramento's Clunie Building in early January 1894, Miss Hazel watched a fight break out between several young toughs on K Street. Thus occupied, she failed to notice a burglar sneak into her room and make off with her purse containing $105 ($3,276 in 2021), including $5 in gold, and a receipt for a parachute she purchased in Seattle.[70]

One Who Walked Away

With 70 parachute jumps to his credit by April 1889, Prof. W.H. Leroy explained his success: "I appreciate the dangers of my undertakings, for out of twelve men engaged in the business last year, seven met their deaths. You see, I was a tight ropewalker and a trapeze artist before I went into the balloon business. I have done so much work in the air that I am like a bird now—live as well in the sky as on land. For the first hundred yards of the fall before the chute opens, you drop like a shot. During this time, you hold your breath. The air roars in your ears, the blood rushes to your head, and you experience the awful sensation of one who dreams he is falling over a precipice. The motion becomes slower, you regain your breath, and it takes all the intelligence you have to watch where you are drifting. There is no such thing as safety. I always take chances of a fall, of smashing into a tree, or crashing into a forest. When I light on the ground, I generally roll over half a dozen times before I recover my equilibrium." (*Ft. Worth Daily Gazette*, April 27, 1890, "Rather Dangerous.")

11

Fiery Fisticuffs & Lamentable Losses

Miss Hazel performed at Elsinore, California, in the spring of 1894, before traveling to Los Angeles for a show at Westlake Park (now MacArthur Park) with Miss Jennie Yan Yan and Prof. Romig. One evening, the trio set out to visit friends in the upscale Boyle Heights neighborhood. The delicious May night held promise of yet another splendid Southern California soiree. However, en route to their engagement, the human element battled over an undisclosed problem. In an abrupt and violent eruption, Prof. Romig thumped Miss Hazel to the ground![71]

To her fine fortune, Officer Dyke witnessed the assault and placed Prof. Romig under arrest. Surprisingly, the lawman permitted him to continue with Miss Hazel to their friends' home.

AMUSEMENTS.

THREE BALLOON ASCENSIONS and TRIPLE PARACHUTE JUMPS

WESTLAKE PARK
AT 4 P.M. SHARP,
Tuesday and Saturday, May 15 and 19
—BY—
MISS HAZEL KEYES
And the Famous Monkey, JENNIE YAN YAN
Thursday, May 17,
—BY—
MISS KEYES, PROF. ROMIG
AND THE MONKEY.
Each will descend from the clouds in a separate parachute.   5-19 7t

Los Angeles Herald, May 15, 1894

Once there, Officer Dyke ordered Romig to the police station, but he vehemently objected. A *Los Angeles Herald* reporter captured the excitement. "Striking a pugilistic attitude," Romig swung "at the officer, almost getting in an effective blow." True to form—tough—like nails—Miss Hazel jumped the fray in a rage, grabbing the officer round the gut "with the tenacity of a bullpup." Fueling the lunacy, a man with a scantling (a piece of timber) rushed forth "to brain the officer."[72]

Officer Dyke escaped the attack and delivered a sharp crack atop Romig's head with his handcuffs, which called brief halt to the proceedings. Aiming his pistol at the chap with the scantling and smiling at Miss Hazel, the officer demanded the skirmish cease. At that moment, while his wife held tight to Dyke, Romig saw his chance to flee. He raced through the friends' house and disappeared out the back door. Freedom proved short-lived, however, when Officer Segger captured the parachuting abuser the following day and chucked him into the local lockup. Lawmen searched for Miss Hazel for several days. When she

The Los Angeles Police team posed with their rifles for this 1890 portrait.
(CHS-31067, https://doi.org/10.25549/chs-m20264)

appeared, at last, at police headquarters to inquire about Romig, officers arrested her without incident. The Prof. earned a $10 fine for battering his wife while she went free to make parachute jumps with Miss Jennie Yan Yan. Pointing out the "great many ups and downs in the life of a balloonist," the *Herald* reporter snickered, "[Professor Romig] is at present having one of the downs not upon the programme."[73]

North of San Diego, the La Jolla Park Hotel's struggling owners, Frank Botsford and George Heald, engaged Miss Hazel's electrifying act to stimulate business. She entertained crowds with three parachute jumps a day. On June 17, 1894, she ascended before 1,000 people and landed in rough Pacific Ocean waters 300 yards from the Boomer Beach shore. She used the life preserver she always carried with her when near water to ride the powerful waves until men rescued her. Perhaps due to the violent dust-up with Prof. Romig, Miss Hazel next took on A.W. Graham as her manager. Graham booked her for a double parachute jump with Miss Jennie Yan Yan at Los Angeles' Athletic Park for the "Benson Benefit" in September 1894.[74]

A thousand merrymakers joined the Athletic Park fun. Capped by a triumphant double-balloon ascension and skydive, the day filled with bicycle, horse, and foot races, leaving all well-satisfied. Always willing to share her story, when a reporter asked Miss Hazel to describe the feeling of diving toward the ground from incredible heights, she responded: "The sensations are diametrically opposite to the general idea that prevails among people who never made such [an] attempt. Instead of feeling yourself lifted bodily and swiftly up into space, you have a realistic sense of staying just exactly where you were and of the earth falling away and downward from you. When it comes to a standstill, you realize for the first time that you have removed upward," she continued. "Of course, the wonderful panorama spread out below you gives you instant advice of the immense altitude you have attained."[75]

"The descent from such a tremendous height by the parachute is another thing, though it, too, involves something of the same sensation, reversed," maintained Miss Hazel. "Until the parachute fills,

[it] is as sheer and sudden and direct as any unpremeditated fall you ever experienced, ranging in depth, according to the volume of wind, from 25 to 100 feet. This is the most unpleasant part of my business. The same precaution of holding the breath is as imperatively necessary in this first fall as it is when you are submerged in the water. In default of such precaution, you are equally liable to strangulation as beneath the water. You seem to see the earth ascending to meet you, but your progress downward is so gentle and so much more deliberate after the parachute opens that you cannot but know you are going down."

Queried about her longest parachute jump, Miss Hazel hearkened back to her 1890 Baker Beach performance outside the Golden Gate Bridge at San Francisco. She told of making one "perfectly successful" jump from an altitude of just over 2½ miles "as determined by mathematical instruments." That day, she dropped into the San Francisco Bay's icy waters wearing a life preserver, and a boatman swooped in to haul her from the brine. Miss Hazel explained, "The easiest place to land is a body of water or a plowed field." Preferring the field at first, she would come to favor landing in the water after ankle injuries took their toll.[76]

Following their Los Angeles performance, Miss Hazel and her monkey traveled east to Yuma, Arizona, where the unthinkable occurred. Though "dodgers" (handbills) advertised the duo's November 25, 1894 parachute jump, the town's *Arizona Sentinel* printed a cryptic announcement: "The monkey is lost, but 'Bow' is hunting a substitute." Indeed, Miss Jennie Yan Yan had disappeared! Crushed at having lost her beloved pet, Miss Hazel initiated a frantic, fruitless search of the Colorado River town. Heartbroken but knowing that the show should proceed, she replaced her companion with a dog. Strapped to its parachute, the canine ascended and landed safely.[77]

The aerial star tried a different tactic to excite her flock at Phoenix in March 1895—shooting off fireworks while parachuting at night. The *Arizona Republican* claimed, "This is a feat never attempted by a female aeronaut and practiced by only one other member of the aerial craft." Her Saturday program went well. On Sunday evening, however, Miss Hazel barely avoided death. At 600 feet, she fired a rocket

Yuma Main Street Water Treatment Plant, Jones Street at the foot of Main Street, Yuma, Arizona ca. 1890s. (*https://www.loc.gov/pictures/item/az0293. photos.041608p*)

that punctured her balloon, setting it ablaze. Air shot from the bag as it crumpled, and a south wind pushed the sizzling affair toward Phoenix's Insane Asylum at Twenty-Fourth and Van Buren Streets.[78]

Keyes plunged to earth as fire devoured the limp ghost of her balloon. A telephone wire broke her fall slightly, but she lay in the dirt unconscious for three hours until searchers

THIS TIME BY FIRE.

Hazel Keyes Has Another Narrow Escape.

Her Balloon Is Set on Fire by a Rocket at a Height of Six Hundred Feet.

Hazel Keyes, the aeronaut, had an exciting experience and a narrow escape from a horrible death on Sunday night. She gave an exhibition at the park, the ascension involving the new feature of a display of fireworks in mid-

Arizona Republican (Phoenix), March 19, 1895

located her around midnight. Phoenix's *Arizona Republican* headline shouted, "This Time by Fire," recounting her frightening landing in the torrents of the Salt River just two months earlier. Declaring her injuries "not supposed to be serious," the newspaper added, "The aeronaut had an exciting experience and a narrow escape from a horrible death."[79]

Gone in a flash at Yuma, Arizona, Miss Jennie Yan Yan clutched a ring in Salem, Oregon's Trover-Cronise Studio for this 1893 photo. Reports of this Miss Jennie Yan Yan rejoining her in performances failed to surface, and Miss Hazel employed other animals, including a new monkey, in future shows. (Oregon Historical Society A-886)

12

Vicious Jealousy & Sailing New Territory

Miss Hazel rebounded from her flaming Phoenix fiasco, and citizens in Yuma, Arizona, looked forward to her performing at their 1895 Fourth of July celebration. She agreed to have a new balloon sewn if the planning committee could provide her with the fabric. At the same time, Kingman, Arizona leaders expressed dismay, believing that they had already secured the Parachute Queen for their Independence Day festivities. "That young lady went back on her contract," railed the *Mohave County Miner*.[80]

Instead of performing in either town, Miss Hazel boarded a ship bound for Guaymas, Sonora, Mexico, in July 1895. Two months later, the still balloonless, steel-willed aeronaut returned with her son Eddie to Nogales, Arizona, where they took a room in the Bowman Hotel. One night, horror rained down upon Miss Hazel while she slept. When a young man she'd met, George Thompson, grew jealous of her flirting with other men, he snuck into her hotel room. Fiendishly drunk on mescal, the Tombstone, Arizona fellow stabbed her in the chest with a knife three times. Miss Hazel did not yell for help but fought with savagery as blood seeped from her wounds. Awakened, her son raced to alert Hotel Manager Wolf, who burst into the room and grabbed the soused assailant. Thompson then sliced his own throat from ear to ear, believing he had killed his paramour, but only inflicting flesh wounds.[81]

The *Tombstone Epitaph's Arizona Kicker* expressed no compassion for Miss Hazel, praising her attacker as a "well and favorab[ly] known [man] in Tombstone." The well-liked Thompson worked many years as a teamster for J. V. Durkee & Co. A member of Tombstone's Patriotic Sons of America and a "young man of exemplary habits, [he] was respected by all who knew him. He has a mother and a brother living in Tombstone who have the sympathy of the community in their great sorrow. Surely his lines must have fell [sic] in evil places to have caused him to commit the rash act." Treated and released, Miss Hazel soon crossed the border into Arizona.[82]

Miss Hazel recuperated from her Nogales stabbing for an entire year before returning to skydiving. Traveling to the American Midwest and outfitted with a new balloon made in Sioux City, Iowa, she scheduled performances at nearby Crystal Lake, Nebraska. As she and a new "Monkey Wonder Jennie Yan Yan" readied for their September 6, 1896 flight, the smell of burning fuel hung over the largest crowd ever assembled at the lake. Crazy cranked up when a nervous Ed H. Monahan arrived to ascend with Miss Hazel. The Sioux City Metropolitan Block elevator operator agreed to purchase an old balloon from her if that day's ride in the sky met his expectations. The Iowa native hustled about nattily dressed in a sweater and short trousers, helping prepare for the scheduled ascension. However, Monahan faced stirring defiance when his mother and wife arrived in a buggy with Sioux City, Iowa Police Chief James Nelson. Acting as a family friend rather than a law officer, Nelson jumped in to prevent the flight.[83]

As the balloon filled with hot air, Chief Nelson and Monahan tussled. St. Joseph, Missouri's *Weekly Gazette* reporter chuckled: "When Nelson was through with [the husband], the bystanders were unable to piece [him] together in time for the balloon ascension." Claiming assault, the victim obtained a warrant for Nelson's arrest, but the Chief quickly slipped back across the Missouri River into Iowa. Miss Hazel carried professional parachutist Professor John Deering into the air instead. Events took an even wilder turn the following Sunday when she went aloft with laundryman A. Hirbour's big black bear! Eating popcorn in peace beforehand, "Bruno" appeared terrified as the balloon lifted off, flailing its paws wildly. The balloon rocketed higher after Miss Hazel cut the bear loose, spurring anxiety among the massive crowd about her safety. She and her ursine companion landed without injury, however. Despite its owner having borrowed a revolver from the local police station, in case the bear got "ugly" after the descent, he found Bruno munching corn in a nearby field.[84]

America's Pioneer Parachute Queen staged a balloon race with Prof. Deering at Crystal Lake to great fanfare that September. Miss Hazel's fame grew when newspapers as far away as New Jersey and Pennsylvania touted the race as the first "ever held in the world." Pre-event advertising claimed that the pair "have been rivals for a long time, and the race is to a great extent the outcome of a long-standing dispute

TO RACE IN BALLOONS.

A Fair Aeronaut Will Try to Beat Her Male Rival In the Air.

SIOUX CITY, Ia., Sept. 19.—What contestants say will be the first balloon race ever held in the world is scheduled to take place at Crystal Lake, Neb., this afternoon, between Professor Deering and Miss Hazel Keyes, both of this city.

These two aeronauts have been rivals for a long time, and the race is to a great extent the outcome of a long standing dispute concerning their respective merits as balloonists. The balloons will be liberated

The Courier-News (Bridgewater, New Jersey), September 19, 1896

concerning their respective merits as balloonists." A referee judged each aeronaut on their balloon's rate of ascension, the height it reached, the speed their parachute dropped, the distance they landed from the point of departure, and, intriguingly, "the behavior of the rival aeronauts." Prof. Deering landed first due to his greater weight to take the victory, and a satisfied crowd dispersed, ready to take their evening meals.[85]

Sioux Falls, South Dakota's Tri-State Fair next hosted Miss Hazel and her monkey. A local news story reported that she "hangs suspended by her teeth alone" and "performs with two trapeze [bars] held ten feet apart by an iron bar and makes daring leaps from one to the other." Seeking to maintain peak interest in her performance, Miss Hazel began ferrying dogs, cats, and other animals with her and parachuting them to earth. She agreed to perform "every day of the week—barring fatal accident." Touted here as the "Queen of Cloudland," Miss Hazel soared to about a mile above the turf, cut free of the balloon, and landed safely in the river bottom along the railroad tracks toward Milwaukee, Wisconsin. Remaining in the nation's midsection, she showcased her skills at Nebraska's Burlington Beach that October before enjoying a winter hiatus.[86]

After a several-month respite, Miss Hazel and Prof. James J. Romig headed into the South in 1897. She and Miss Jennie Yan Yan parachuted in Birmingham, Alabama, on June 6. She took a goose up with her monkey as 2,000 people filled the grounds at North Birmingham Park. The goose's parachute floated to earth without difficulty, and E.F. Dill returned it to the North Birmingham Street Railway Company to collect the $3 reward Miss Hazel offered for its return.

Terror reigned, however, when Miss Hazel couldn't slice the rope tethering her parachute to the balloon, and it failed to open. She slammed against a tree as she came to earth three miles from the park. Unconscious and severely bruised, she almost smothered when the balloon landed atop her. Three local men rushed to extract her and took her into town in a buggy. Due to the injuries, Prof. Romig and Miss Jennie performed without the aerial queen four days later. Undaunted,

Miss Hazel flew again in a double parachute jump at the city's Fourth of July celebration. Romig offered up his most incredible stunt on July 5 when he ascended in the balloon with Miss Hazel to a "dizzy height," and she shot him from a cannon with his parachute! While the outcome of the Prof.'s explosive ride went unreported, a Professor Koko took the next cannon-shot ride with Miss Hazel's help. That pair followed up with a July 15 balloon flight displaying fireworks. Miss Hazel then left Birmingham and headed to Tennessee for shows with Miss Jennie Yan Yan in Chattanooga in late August 1897.[87]

Reports of Miss Hazel's performances faded until the summer of 1898, when she made several ascensions in Austin, Texas. In mid-July, she posted a newspaper advertisement—"A Man Wanted"—seeking an unmarried newspaper fellow willing to take the air with her. The offer included a light-hearted guarantee to "bring him back to *terra firma* safely or no charge for services."[88]

Birmingham, Alabama streetcars converge in front of Mayor A.O. Lane's mansion at a corner of 8th Avenue and 9th Street in this period image. (https:// commons.wikimedia.org/wiki/File:The_street_railway_review_(1891)_(14757403911).jpg)

Sunday, July 4th, at 5 P. M.

Go to North Birmingham Park, July 5, to

SEE THE GREATEST AND GRANDEST ATTRACTIONS OF THE DAY.

Sack Race, Wheelbarrow Race, Greasy Pole, Tub Race, Goat Race, Greasy Pig. Also Grand Balloon Ascension and Cannon Leap by Prof. J. J. ROMIG, who will make a Grand Balloon Ascension, and at a dizzy height will be shot from a cannon attached to the balloon and descend in a parachute, assisted by Miss Hazel Keyes.

Trains leave First avenue and Nineteenth Street every 15 minutes

FREE! FREE! FREE!

GOOD MUSIC FOR DANCING DAY AND NIGHT.

The Birmingham News (Alabama), July 2, 1897

Austin Tribune writer, E.H. Eves, came forward despite numerous public predictions that he would fold in fear before his ascent. Whole-hearted applause greeted Eves as he entered the circle of people surrounding Miss Hazel's balloon. The reporter had prepared for his sky ride by "practicing athletics to develop his muscles and drinking copiously of all obtainable nerve tonics." Bessere's Orchestra played for excited excursionists as the steamer *Ben Hur* pulled into place on the lake to give the best view of the performance. Eves and Miss Hazel adjusted their positions beneath the balloon, and with her "Let go," they made for the heavens. At about 1,000 feet, she sent the journalist off with his parachute. He landed safely in the lake, eschewed a boat ride, and swam to shore unaided.[89]

Now reporting more than 700 ascensions and touted as "the greatest living female aeronaut," when Miss Hazel cut loose from her balloon, she drifted too close to the Austin Dam. Swinging her body back and forth in frenzied effort, she battled to force the parachute over it. Aware of disaster's imminence, the sky-flier made yet another miraculous escape, flying just over the dam's crest rather than slamming headlong into it. Many spectators worried she'd hit the downstream face of the wall, and hundreds sprinted to the barrier's far side in search of their parachuting darling. "Such a race of humanity was probably never before witnessed in Texas," declared a local writer. Just below the toe of the dam, Miss Hazel fought to stay afloat within a turbulent eddy in the middle of the stream as her parachute engulfed her. In mortal combat with her stringy lifesaver, she spotted three young men who had helped hold down her balloon before takeoff swimming towards her. Strong hands soon freed her from the rope prison and escorted the aeronaut to shore uninjured. Rousing cheers and congratulatory handshakes met her and Eves, both dripping wet.[90]

The Austin event marked the fourth time she had taken a reporter up with her, and she called Eves "undoubtedly the coolest" of the four. She declared that he showed "plenty of grit and determination" and demonstrated "the greatest amount of disregard for any possible danger." America's special skyrobat detailed their flight. "Mr. Eves did his part most splendidly in making it a successful performance. Away he went, straight into the water, saluting with his cap as he fell. I knew he was safe. Then it was my turn to 'take a tumble.' I thought sure I was going to strike the dam, but by hard work, I just barely managed to miss the edge of the granite wall." Once down, "I got all tangled up in the parachute ropes and was very glad to be helped out."

Texas' newest journalist-skydiver rendered his enthusiastic account, "To tell the truth, I was really sorry it was over. It had been talked about so much and had so many dangers pictured for me that I was somewhat afraid I was going to be frightened. But I don't believe I got one bit so. I had unlimited confidence in two people. Miss Keyes, whom I considered thoroughly expert in her line of business, and myself. So, why should I get frightened? I never saw a balloon ascension until Miss Keyes made one on the Fourth of July, and now I have made one. I am ready to make another at any time."[91]

A fellow columnist congratulated Eves on "having disappointed so many people who were predicting that he would back out." The writer also saluted Miss Hazel's expertise, "She is an artist in her chosen profession. It is a rather risky thing to take with her on such a perilous trip a man who has never had a similar experience. That she brought him back in safety and anxious to make another ascension is a good testimonial to her thoroughness with which she does her work."[92]

Oft willing to extend her entertainment scheme's limits, Miss Hazel's next Austin gambit might well have topped her list of antics—a "blood curdling" slide down a seven-strand steel cable suspended by her hair with a wire. On September 4, 1898, she planned to ride 1,000 feet from the summit of Mount Bonnell over Lake McDonald to the Austin Dam powerhouse with her new Miss Jennie Yan Yan perched atop her back. That afternoon, as the steamer *Ben Hur* chugged across the lake loaded with excited passengers, workers strapped the cable to a large oak tree atop Mt. Bonnell, then fastened the wire around Miss Hazel's hair.[93]

Charging down the cable at lightning velocity, she dropped Miss Jennie Yan Yan into the water with her parachute and continued her descent. As she approached the powerhouse on the lake's other side, too much slack in the cable prohibited the hair-bound daredevil from reaching it. Miss Hazel hung suspended above the water before men in a boat arrived and threw her a rope. Executing her fantastical ride without reported injuries to herself or her monkey, Miss Hazel earned permanent recognition on a metal historical marker at Mt. Bonnell's base. In addition, the Tobin Drug Company gave her a bottle of extract, and the Austin Jewelry & Loan Association presented her with a pair of silver garters. A local correspondent declared, "The wonderful feat will be given [again] to afford the patrons the opportunity of seeing the greatest of all performances ever seen in Texas before Miss Keyes leaves the city." Several months after her Austin performances, Miss Hazel filed suit against the Dummy Railroad Line for undiscovered reasons. Almost a year later, Justice Stuart tossed out her case because "being a married woman, the plaintiff could not bring suit in her own name."[94]

The 1900 Collapse of Lake McDonald

Formed by the construction of Austin Dam in 1890–1893. Austin, Texas' Lake McDonald disappeared on April 7, 1900. After spectacular storms drove floodwaters 11 feet over the top of the dam, a thundering snap "like a gunshot" echoed across the Texas town at 11:20 a.m. The central section of the dam collapsed in a concrete tumble, leaving only its west end intact and Austin without electricity for months. Rebuilt as the Tom Miller Dam in 1940, some chunks of the original structure remain as parts of the Red Bud Isles today. (Bruce Hunt, *notevenpast.com*, "The Rise and Fall of the Austin Dam," July 9, 2011)

Nearby homes lie in shambles following the collapse of the Austin Dam on April 7, 1900. (https://lccn.loc.gov/2014689748)

This weathered plaque at Mt. Bonnell honors Miss Hazel Keyes' incredible glide down a cable in 1898. (https://commons.wikimedia.org/wiki/ File:Mt-Bonnell_1860_rs.png)

13

Esau the Snake Eater & An Aerial Legend Settles to Ground

Miss Hazel made several parachuting exhibitions in Austin in October 1898 before performing at county fairs in north Texas and Oklahoma. After an ascension at Ft. Worth with her monkey in December 1899, the pair gave another at Houston, Texas, in August 1900. That November, Safford, Arizona, beckoned, and advertisements pictured her and her current monkey parachuting above the tag line: "Bring all the snakes and Gila Monsters you can find and see Esau, The Snake Eater." Adding another dimension to their performance, Prof. Romig promoted the famous East Indian snake muncher. Billed as the

Graham Guardian (Safford, Az.), November 23, 1900

"J.J. Romig Snake Show," Esau performed several shows in Clifton, Arizona, before coming to Safford.[95]

With her ascent's preparations completed, Miss Hazel took the air and rose several hundred feet when her balloon exploded with a deafening boom! Prof. Romig and her sons screamed for her to cut herself free. She spotted smoke billowing from the balloon and fought to direct her parachute from beneath it. The flaming airbag skimmed the parachute as it fell, but Miss Hazel steered it to a safe landing, adding one more harrowing narrow miss to her credit. Safford's *Graham Guardian* writer declared, "Although the sight was a grand one, it was a narrow escape for Miss Keyes. Had the balloon struck the parachute, the balloonist would have come to earth like a rock."[96]

Miss Hazel's woes proceeded unabated following the fiery ascension. After her son Eddie left the table while the family dined in a local restaurant, he never returned. When Prof. Romig returned to the family's tent, he found his valise cut open and $40 stolen. Missing for two days, Eddie and a Safford boy turned up in the small town of Bowie, 50 miles to the south on the Southern Pacific Railroad line, having spent part of the money. Miss Hazel corralled her errant boy and headed for a scheduled performance at Phoenix's Carnival. However, without her balloon, only the J.J. Romig Snake Show, with its viper-eating star, Esau, made the date.[97]

America's premier female aerialist executed her final series of ascensions during Prescott, Arizona's 1901 Independence Day celebration. Her favorite balloon done up in the Safford blaze the previous fall, Miss Hazel owned a 60-foot-tall secondary balloon but stood reluctant to trust such a small affair at Prescott's 5,368-foot elevation. The city's Knights of Pythias Hall whirred with action and anticipation late that June. Prescott women kept three new sewing machines running each day and part of the night, helping to stitch a massive new cloth apparatus for Keyes. The daring parachutist's new balloon stood 80 feet in circumference, contained more than 800 yards of muslin, and required "more than a few miles of sewing to complete." Wise to the ways of commerce, Miss Hazel offered the chance to advertise on the side of her balloon to the highest bidder. No reported takers emerged, however. Miss Hazel, now around 40, planned to climb to one mile and hover there for 30 minutes before her parachute jump. She brought two prodigious lizards to Arizona's Mile High City performance, but both disappeared. Instead, she fastened Palace Saloon owner Bob Brow's pet raccoon to a basket and released it in a small parachute. Miss Hazel "is highly spoken of as a lady and is certainly one of the prettiest mid-air performers ever seen hanging to a balloon," crowed a local scribe.[98]

Smoke billowed from a furnace in the southeast corner of the city plaza at 7:40 p.m. on July 4, 1901. As she always did, Miss Hazel worked beside her helpers to inflate her new balloon while 20 strong men fought to secure the bloated behemoth. She strapped herself to the trapeze bar when it filled to over two-thirds. On her "Goodbye all; let her go," the bag shot skyward to around 3,500 feet, where winds drove it east from the plaza. When America's Parachute Queen crashed to earth, her chute drug her through a thicket of bushes, scratching her face. Three men on horseback raced to assist her, helped retrieve her balloon, and returned her to Prescott. Given her gregarious nature, one might imagine a raucous and bawdy night at "Bob Brow's Palace and Not Ashamed of It" following her arrival.[99]

Miss Hazel flew the next night and again floated eastward on the wind. Releasing her parachute much earlier than on her previous flight, she dove for about 150 feet before it opened without a problem. Swinging back and forth, she struggled to direct her flight toward a safe landing spot. Gusts propelled her over the gulch east of the city's Citizen's Cemetery before slamming her to earth and causing severe sprains to both ankles. Helped into R.E. Morrison's carriage, she returned to central Prescott, where Dr. McNally tended to her injuries. An *Arizona Weekly Journal-Miner* editorial declared, "In view of her accident, the committee would not be censured for canceling the engagement for this evening and paying her the full sum agreed upon for the three evenings." Despite her painful ankle injuries and against the counsel of friends, the audacious sky-flyer kept her commitment and completed the engagement's final parachute jump the following day. Calmer winds allowed her to rise vertically. Cutting free at about 4,000 feet, she landed safely in a flat, open area without rocks or shrubs southwest of Whipple Reservoir.[100]

Following her final performance, Miss Hazel held "a sort of open-air reception" at the brand new Hotel Burke, where esteemed Colonel J.F. Wilson made a brief statement thanking her for her contribution to the city's festivities. Across the dusty street from the hotel, former Chaparral, Arizona postmaster Harry B. Hanna and his wife Caroline cuddled their daughters, Grace and Maude. As the party gained steam, their sons, Frank and Ernest Graham, strolled to a nearby saloon to grab a cool drink. Harry joined in the applause for Miss Hazel, despite his disdain for Wilson, who had shorted him and his workers money for work they'd completed. Contrary to "a move on foot" to engage Miss Hazel for an ascent on the first anniversary of Prescott's devastating July 14, 1900, Great Fire, she quit the aerial game. No further reports of her performances surfaced, and America's Queen of Cloudland announced plans to reside in Prescott. More than a decade would pass before her skydiving days again found the spotlight.[101]

At this point, the reader might pause to ponder which modern-day forms of entertainment demand such frequent recovery from injury. The rigors of American football, bronc and bull riding, hockey, and football (soccer) might advance such a physical challenge. Mid-to-late 20th-century enthusiasts might recall the daring, self-brutalizing canyon, building, and other leaps of famed showman Evel Knievel, which required similar healing. Now, more than a century after her wild rides through the sky, Miss Hazel Keyes' "production" during her career stands Hall of Fame worthy, especially in light of her repeated recovery from injuries with treatment from late-1800s-trained physicians using century-old medical techniques combined with regular "no serious damage" diagnoses following lengthy periods of unconsciousness.

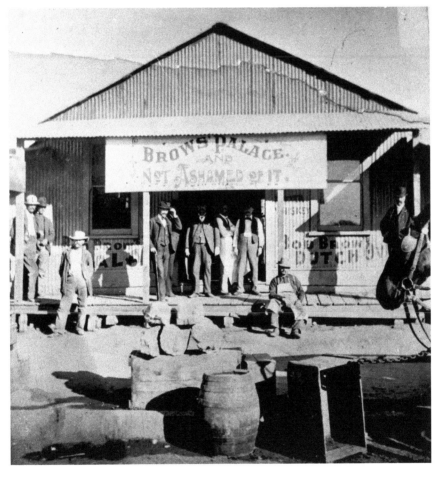

Several pioneers gathered in front of "Bob Brow's Palace and Not Ashamed of It" for this 1900 image just after Prescott's July 14 Great Fire. Brow's pet raccoon parachuted in Miss Hazel's show the following year. (Sharlot Hall Museum, 1400.8011.0002)

14

Sizzling Prescott Passions Foster Rough Play

Prof. James J. Romig took work at William Clark's United Verde Smelter at Jerome (above) following his parachuting career. A major copper producer in Arizona, the smelter closed about 1915 when the United Verde Copper Mine switched to an open-pit operation. (http://hdl.loc.gov/loc.pnp/ds.08171)

Miss Hazel Keyes followed through on her decision to remain in Prescott and earned Yavapai County, Arizona, resident status after living there for one year. While her husband, Prof. James J. Romig, worked in the United Verde Copper Company smelter at Jerome, she reportedly adopted a lifestyle brimming with debauchery. When copper matte from one of the smelter's ore converters scalded Romig, he lay near death in the company's Jerome hospital for seven weeks.

At Miss Hazel's request, and after much coaxing, he came to live with her in Prescott. Dismayed by the abominable routine he discovered, Romig sued for divorce, charging "gross excesses, cruel treatment, and outrage towards" him. He swore that "nearly every morning about six o'clock a.m." his wife checked to make sure he and her child, 11-year-old Eddie, remained asleep, then snuck "from the bed clad only in her nightclothes and sometimes a skirt thrown [around] them." She then slipped "out from the house and into the next house to carouse, drink intoxicants, and consort with various men, bartenders by occupation, who would arrive from their work at about that hour."[102]

His wife "would remain for upwards of an hour with her derelict barkeep associates and, at times, public prostitutes," read Romig's court submission. Further, she "consorts with and is frequently in the company of women who are notorious public characters of highly unsavory reputation and invites them and entertains them." When one indiscreet fellow displayed "a certain picture of such an obscene and filthy character it would not be proper here to describe," she dismissed it, the beleaguered husband contended. "Far from being shocked thereat or angry at the man for doing so," she embarrassed Romig by sharing the incident with a woman, then laughing it off and telling him, "He [the man] was only a little full [drunk] when he did it." The Prof. claimed that Miss Hazel then "forcibly ejected and drove [him] into the street," his body "a mass of copper burns and sores, barely able to leave his bed and scarcely able to walk." Romig pointed to the "great danger" to his "life and personal health" precipitated by his ouster. At 4:00 p.m. that very afternoon, he filed his divorce petition. For undetermined reasons, the court did not grant this divorce.[103]

Flying in the face of facts, sanity, and a presumed extreme bitterness on both sides, Miss Hazel moved to Jerome to live with her husband within a month of booting him from her Prescott home. In September 1901, the pair rented four rooms in the steep hillside mining town. Still married, the volatile team battled a powerful magnetism in an arena brimming with fondly held rancor, alcohol, and recurrent animosity.

Rocky moments occasionally spilled from the Romig home in loud bursts that autumn before a vicious emotional storm exploded on Christmas Eve. Drunken and venomous, Romig chomped into Mattie's fingers before dumping burning oil on them. The nasty digit-muncher screamed abhorrent names such as "bitch" and "whore" at his injured

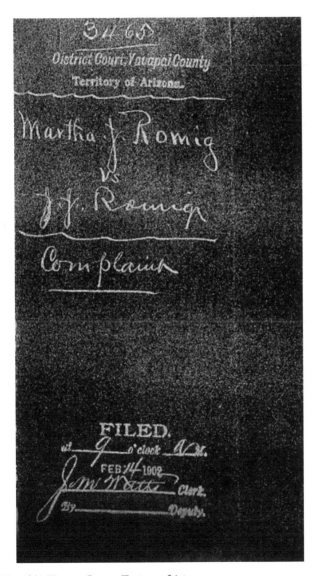

Complaint No. 3465, Yavapai County, Territory of Arizona

wife and followed up with another holiday cursing spree in front of his stepchildren. Her attorney filed suit for divorce on February 14, 1902, charging extreme physical cruelty.[104]

She declared Romig "a man of strong physical constitution and amply able to earn sufficient money to support himself" and his wife. Because "he willfully neglected to provide the actual and common necessities of life," Miss Hazel explained that she felt "compelled to live" on her own earnings. Only conjecture suffices in reckoning the way she collected her funds. Romig's landlord, R.N. Copeland, who shared the Jerome house with the couple, affirmed Miss Hazel's account of the Yuletide assault. After Judge R.E. Sloan granted her a divorce, Miss Hazel Keyes reinvented herself in Los Angeles, California.[105]

15

Husband Three Brings His Own Wild Tale

The spirited bronco bore hard on the bit, clearly bent on bolting. Known as a good driver, Joshua "J.G." De Turk and his worker often trained horses. He'd brought several ponies into line, but this young bay proved more than a handful. A runaway the moment it left the corral, the colt and its spooked mate raced west along Los Angeles' Fort Street at a maddening clip. His wagon careening behind, J.G. braced his feet against a gate at his wagon's front end and its brake, straining to rein in the wild horse. Just as the maverick affair passed several Chinese-owned bathhouses, the gate snapped, hurling De Turk forward onto the wagon's doubletree.[106]

Frantic, J.G. fought to get back into the wagon but lost his balance and slammed head-first onto the street. The wagon rolled over his ankles, and as he raised his head, he saw his outfit crash into a "rickety" old wagon full of wood. In disbelief, he watched as the wagon's coupling pole snapped, throwing one of its front wheels high in the air. His runaway horses then pulled it about 20 feet before racing down the street. Calling his upending a "close call," De Turk escaped "serious, if not fatal injury," but suffered painful bruises to his head, elbows, and legs. Joshua De Turk would endure more than his share of painful, humiliating incidents.[107]

PIONEER AUCTION HOUSE

Of Los Angeles City and County.

First State, County and City License taken out Oct. 1st, 1869, and kept up uninterrupted to the present date.

E. W. NOYES,

GENERAL AUCTIONEER

With J. G. De Turk, No. 1 MARKET St. two doors above Wells, Fargo & Co.'s Office.

Regular Sale Days for horses, carriages, furniture, etc., Wednesdays and Saturdays from 10 o'clock A. M. to 4 o'clock P. M. Cash advances made on consignments. Cash paid for all kinds of goods, wares and merchandise. Charges on the "live and let let live" basis.

N. B.—No real estate sold except by auction. Charges on real estate sales one per cent.

E. W. NOYES, Auctioneer, And General Business Manager for J. G. De Turk. nv21

Los Angeles Herald, December 18, 1878

If parachuting wonder Miss Hazel Keyes led a wild and oft-reported public life during her performing days, Joshua Goodhart De Turk's story might well stand in rank beside hers. Just as Miss Hazel's parachuting career brought incredible highs and painful lows, so De Turk's fortunes climbed the pinnacles, only to shatter on the rocks of despair. Born in Philadelphia on November 14, 1833, J.G. served as a Union Army lieutenant during the Civil War. Moving to Los Angeles, he opened his Livery, Feed, and Sale Stable around 1879. He also owned the Pioneer Auction House at No. 1 Market Street in downtown Los Angeles. J.G. employed veteran auctioneer E. W. Noyes in an astute business move. Noyes' "resonance and timbre of his unrivaled voice" and long-standing credibility bolstered the De Turk enterprise.[108]

As De Turk's affluence blossomed, the politically active Democrat began buying and selling property and improving his investments. While growing his business, J.G. also raced horses. He stood "widely known as one of the keen horse traders of the community," and his half- and quarter-miler, "Walking John," gained local fame.

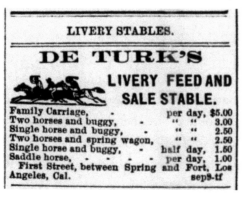

LIVERY STABLES.

DE TURK'S

LIVERY FEED AND SALE STABLE.

Family Carriage, -	per day, $5.00
Two horses and buggy, -	" " 3.00
Single horse and buggy, -	" " 2.50
Two horses and spring wagon,	" " 2.50
Single horse and buggy, -	half day, 1.50
Saddle horse, - - -	per day, 1.00

First Street, between Spring and Fort, Los Angeles, Cal. sep9-tf

Los Angeles Times, July 18, 1882

Well-respected in the community, J.G. served as the International Order of Odd Fellows Lodge No. 35's Noble Grand (N.G.) in 1883. Grand Marshall of the Order's 1887 Grand Parade of Uniformed Knights to the Los Angeles Opera House, De Turk sat among the honored guests during Mayor W.H. Workman's address.[109]

Fifty-two-year-old J.G. De Turk married divorcée Mrs. Mary L. Burdick on May 5, 1885, and mayhem ensued. Infidelity, abuse, and abandonment filled the couple's marital tenure before the dailies shared

Los Angeles Lodge No. 35, I. O. O. F.

REGULAR meeeting held on Wednesday evening of each week at 7:30 o'clock. Sojourning brethren in good standing are cordially invited.

J. G. DE TURK, N. G.

A. FRANK R. S

Los Angeles Herald, June 16, 1883

details in "one of the raciest" divorce proceedings "ever tried in this city." A *Los Angeles Times* story proclaimed, "It is as complete a star-chamber case as has ever taken place in the city." Another added, "Both he and his wife seemed determined to go clear to the bottom." Conflict began in September 1886 when Mary De Turk accused J.G. of consorting with their live-in housekeeper Miss Reynolds.[110]

Intrigue up-stepped after Mary returned from a trip to Iowa with her children and moved into Los Angeles' Hollenbeck Hotel rather than with her husband. J.G. De Turk purchased the City Warehouse on Upper Main Street for $25,000 the following month, but reports of his wife's infidelity rocked his home life. He hired private detective A.B. Lawson, who named several men seen with his wife at the notorious Flag Cottage.

Near the University of Southern California, the calm and reputable community of University Place surrounded the city's unsavory locale. Infamous as a site where married men and women enjoyed "high carnival," the lewd location provided "the means of debauching many women who may have been giddy but were not criminal before," explained a news account. "Not one of the low dives, this is the only place of this kind near the city" and a "thorn in the side of the people. Its gaudy and meretricious

FLAG COTTAGE,

LOS ANGELES,   CALIFORNIA,

**Known as the Old Howes Residence,
one mile from end car line on
Jefferson street.**

NICE GROVE AND BEAUTIFUL DRIVE.

House of fifteen rooms, neatly furnished,
and a pleasant resort.

ALL KINDS OF WINES AND LIQUORS.

THE PUBLIC ARE CORDIALLY INVITED.

Los Angeles Herald, March 8, 1889, "Advertisement."

splendors, for it is gorgeously fitted up," melded "very badly with the sober aspect" of the surrounding homes. "There was never a more dangerous place in the city, morally speaking," declared a *Los Angeles Times* account. Mrs. Mary C. De Turk, a 35-year-old brunette, described as "quite tall with somewhat irregular features," had "kept company" with several men at Flag Cottage during her marriage. When J.G. learned that his wife "consorted affectionately" with Bob Sutherland, a compositor for the *Los Angeles Tribune,* he waited near the Rose Block on North Main Street. As the pair descended a stairway and left the building, J.G. pounced upon Sutherland and choked him.[111]

Despite his home conflicts, J.G. continued his business success, selling his First Street property to the Los Angeles Board of Trade in September 1887 for $100,000 ($2.9 million in 2021). As his marriage troubles escalated, J.G. moved into his employee, M.S. Hartenstein's

AN ODD CONTRACT

**A Board Bill That Kept Mounting Up
All the Time**

J. G. De Turk, the sale and livery stable man, seems to have got into a rather curious trouble, for suit has been brought against him by M. S. Hartenstein and for an unusual cause of action.

Los Angeles Herald, October 13, 1897

home. By February 20, 1893, Hartenstein and his wife Kate had provided De Turk with $1,020 in room, board, and laundry services and had done $410 worth of work for him. In exchange, De Turk

J.G. De Turk demolished the old adobe buildings on the northwest corner of First Street and Fort Street (Broadway Street after 1890) in Los Angeles and constructed his Livery, Feed, and Sale Stable (above), a 160' × 60' brick building, assessed at $15,000 in 1885 ($467,958 in 2021). At the time, $2,500 could buy 10 acres near the city with municipal water or a good well. He sold the property to the Los Angeles Board of Trade for $100,000 in September 1887 ($3,119,721 in 2021). (USCL, CHS, C.C. Pierce Photography CHS-c65-1744, https://doi.org/10.25549/chs-m51)

promised to deed the couple his lot near South Pearl and West Eighth Streets. Trusting him, they constructed a house, planted trees, and completed $945 in improvements on the property. However, J.G. mortgaged the lot for $6,000 to purchase another property, and the Hartensteins filed suit. Though they won a judgment against J.G., their property description proved inaccurate, voiding the decision. Marital strife lingered before the court granted J.G. a divorce in October

1890. Nevertheless, with between $85,000 and $95,000 in the bank ($2.6–$2.7 million in 2021 dollars), he continued to thrive financially and enjoyed the prestige and blessings of wealth. Among his many real estate deals, he granted right-of-way to the Vernon Irrigation Co. across his 14-acre tract south of Los Angeles in December 1891.[112]

The precipitous crash of 60-year-old J.G De Turk proved a dramatic riches-to-rags tale when America's financial Panic of 1893 destroyed his abundance along with the nation's. He defaulted on his mortgages, and poverty engulfed him. The Odd Fellows Golden Rule Lodge No. 35 suspended him in December 1897, perhaps for unpaid dues. His southward spiral gained momentum on the evening of June 4, 1898. Relegated to driving a horse-drawn garbage wagon, J.G. rolled down Temple Street near Belmont Avenue when a streetcar smashed into his rig. The collision shot him six feet into the air and slammed him onto the street.[113]

Severely bruised and shaken, with his wagon crumpled, the once esteemed entrepreneur appeared to drop onto the bottom floor in his dive to desperation the following February. As he rumbled along his garbage collection route, Officer Matuskiewiz arrested J.G. for hauling swill rather than garbage in his wagon. The *Los Angeles Herald* story noted, "The career of De Turk is a sad commentary upon the vicissitudes of fortune. Things went from bad to worse until he was forced to act as a public scavenger." A *Times* writer chimed in, "Much sympathy is felt for De Turk, a man who has been particularly unfortunate. [He] has been reduced to the necessity of collecting garbage as a means of livelihood."[114]

A Licentious Love Hotel

Charles and Maud McCormick ran an assignation house, or Love Hotel, at Flag Cottage. While visitors could rent rooms by the hour, it maintained a semi-respectable air by masquerading as a traveler's inn. Flag Cottage's reputation sent a "flurry of excitement" through Los Angeles' social circles. One columnist declared, "Dame Rumor says many Angelic matrons, who are usually looked upon as the pinks of perfection," visited the establishment. If the facts "had been made public, it would have thrown a number of families in the city into unpleasant notoriety and disgraced certain men and women."

A *Los Angeles Herald* writer added, "The fast men in town needed little direction to find the place. It has been an open secret that high jinks were played there for the past 24 months. Reports have reached the outside world of revels there which would not disgrace the orgies of Bacchantes."

One particularly heinous chap, a Los Angeles County Tax Collector known as "the historic El Hammond," embezzled $9,000 to party at the infamous assignation house. Before disappearing, the "vaquero of malodorous memory" wasted up to $600 on "many a night with his fat and greasy beer-slinging inamorata." The court convicted both McCormicks on charges of operating a "house of ill fame" in May 1889. (*Los Angeles Times*, May 29, 1889, "The Flag Cottage"; *Los Angeles Herald*, March 8, 1889, "The Flag Cottage"; December 17, 1889, "New Cases.")

Joshua De Turk's first wife, Mary De Turk, and her children took residence in Los Angeles' Hollenbeck Hotel after returning from a trip to Iowa. (USCL), [CHS] CHS-2346, https://doi.org/10.25549/chs-m1264)

Far from the "high carnival" at notorious Flag Cottage, horse-drawn carriages and streetcars roll down Los Angeles' Spring Street. The city tripled in population between 1890 and 1900. (USC Libraries, CHS-154.1, https://digitallibrary.usc.edu/asset-management/2A3BF1RZUE4?WS=SearchResults)

16

A Brand New Start in Hog Heaven

Miss Hazel Keyes resurfaced in Los Angeles as a more grounded persona in 1903. Now known as Martha H. "Mattie" Romig, she operated a chicken and duck ranch near the Los Angeles River south of the city. That drama and trauma accompanied her while performing on the balloon/parachute circuit stands certain. The degree to which her aerial game's injuries, trials, and challenges exacted their respective mental, physical, and emotional fees and helped sculpt this feisty, tough, steel-willed, attractive, courageous woman comes into question. Her performance going forward will prove her a sharp and agile businessperson.

For his part, Joshua G. De Turk faded from public view following his downfall until a March 1904 *Los Angeles Times* item mentioned his 14-acre Vernon tract. By the time Mattie met De Turk, he had retooled himself as the "Hog King of Los Angeles." A reserved Pennsylvania Dutchman, 28 years her senior, Joshua's efforts to rebuild his life and fortune affirmed his credo: "No man in this country need be poor, and every man should pay his debts."[115]

Mattie explained that at the beginning of their relationship, J.G. told her about the "money in hogs." Indeed, a *Times* story avers, De Turk "knows the genus hog from the cradle to the grave. He has served that useful animal in every capacity from bottle nurse to undertaker, occasionally pausing to be executioner." Mattie continued, "I did not understand hogs, and every time we met, he talked hogs. After a while, he moved his little home, and I moved mine until they stood side by side. One day he said that the neighbors were speaking ill of me, and the way to stop it was to get married."

Though some might question the union's rationale, Mattie, about 43, wed the 70-year-old Civil War veteran in Los Angeles on April 7, 1904. The fabled aeronaut of flash and crash, Miss Hazel Keyes, would hide her former persona from the community and her husband for more than 10 years until a newspaper story revealed her prior identity. Perhaps destined for each other based on their colorful pasts, they would double down on the crazy during their 11-year marriage. "We were partners. I gave him $800, and he put up $600, and we bought the property we have now [14 acres along the Los Angeles River at 2600 George Street in Vernon]."[116]

State of California   County of Los Angeles

Marriage License

These Presents *Are to authorize and license any Justice of the Supreme Court, Judge of the Superior Court, Justice of the Peace, Priest or Minister of the Gospel of any denomination, to solemnize within said County,*
the marriage of *Joshua J. De Surk* native of *Pennsylvania*
aged *70* years, resident of *Los Angeles* County of *Los Angeles*
State of California, and *Martha Hazel Roennig* native of *California*
aged *42* years, resident of *Los Angeles* County of *Los Angeles*
State of California, said parties being of sufficient age to be capable of contracting marriage.
IN WITNESS WHEREOF, I have hereunto set my hand and affixed the seal of the Superior
[SEAL] *Court of said County, this* 6 *day of* April *A. D. 190* 4
C. G. KEYES,
County Clerk and ex-officio Clerk of the Superior Court in and for said Los Angeles County.
By W. B. Watson *Deputy Clerk.*

STATE OF CALIFORNIA, } ss. *I hereby certify that I believe the facts stated in the within and above License*
County of Los Angeles, *to be true, and that upon due inquiry there appears to be no legal impediment to the marriage of said.*
Joshua J. De Surk and Martha Hazel Roennig that said parties were joined
in marriage by me on the seventh *day of* April *190* 4 *in the city said County and State;*
that Gilbert L. Dennison *a resident of* said city *County of*
Los Angeles State of California and H. E. McAfee
a resident of said city *County of* Los Angeles *State of* California
were present as witnesses of said ceremony.
I have hereunto set my hand this seventh *day of* April *A. D. 190* 4
762. B. N. Smith, Judge of the Superior
A full, true and correct copy of the original, recorded this 12 *day of* Apr. *190* 4
at 5 P. M. at request of Judge
CALVIN HARTWELL, County Recorder.
By H. Grossman *Deputy.*

Los Angeles County, Public Records, https://www.familysearch.org/ark:/61903/3:1:939Z-BV9B-TT?i=408&cc=1804002

The De Turk hog ranch prospered, and Mattie held firm charge of the family business operation and the money. One day, a teamster stopped at the De Turk's with a wagon full of tin cans and offered her 25 cents to dump his load on their property. Other drivers then agreed to pay her to take wagonloads of sand from the riverbed. Soon, a regular flow of wagons loaded with cans arrived each day and hauled away sand. She explained, "I couldn't understand why my sand was in such strong demand until I learned that the older pits along the river were becoming exhausted. Also, structures and other improvements farther up the river were making the sand more and more inaccessible. When I first permitted men to haul sand from my land, it was to let them make a hole to bury the cans. Now, the teamsters are paying me for the privilege of making a burial place for them, all of which is very lovely. We got money coming and going."

Locally renowned, Mattie earned the moniker "Los Angeles Sand-Lot Queen." A *Times* scribe noted, "All the owner has to do is rake in the nickels and order up her motor car. The only equipment that she uses is a pencil, a notebook, and a big purse. She doesn't need a bookkeeper because everybody is required to pay cash. At first thought, it does not seem possible for anyone to become wealthy selling sand at 15 cents a load"; however, she took in more than $1,000 ($31,195 in 2021) a month. At one point, Mattie declared, "It's a little dull. Only about 200 wagons a day are calling for sand now." She also began accepting garbage to feed her hogs.[117]

Fires kept burning on the ranch to incinerate the tons of paper that arrived each day, created an eerie, surreal sense when a correspondent visited the De Turk ranch one spring evening. Absorbing its bristly scene, the journalist wrote: "On a dark night, the place looks as if an isolated hamlet had just been devastated by fire and the inhabitants had fled." Despite its riverside setting, the hog ranch created one of Southern California's most loathsome olfactory locations. "Take the Mateo streetcar to the end of the line and there sniff the air," explains the scribe. "Then, follow your nose, or rather force your nose in the right direction, for any self-respecting nose would quickly run away if it could. The weak stomach begins to feel very rebellious when within a few blocks of the place."

Ritual governed the De Turks' hog husbandry. A ravenous swine troop spent its daytimes wallowing, tussling, and snoozing in a large enclosure with only drinking water. After J.G. closed the rubbish realm's entrance gates each evening at dusk, he released 50 famished hogs. The fatsome brutes rushed upon a goldmine of decaying fish, chickens, and swill. California's City of Angels held no prohibition against using swill to fatten hogs. On another ranch section, 50 more swine dined on vast piles of rotting fruit and vegetables from local markets and factories. The gluttonous grunters gorged on so much of the questionable nutrition that Joshua declared he often needed to thin down the hogs when they reached market age.[118]

Wastings in the city's butcher shops received a chloride of lime "dressing" before their trip to the dump, and each morning, workers found three to seven dead hogs that stuck their snouts into the chemically-dosed rubbish piles. In addition, young pigs often died after accidentally eating the fine glass restaurant workers swept off floors into their garbage cans. Hog King Joshua De Turk labeled these deaths a cost of doing business. Amidst the chemical-laden offal, scavenging humans dined on grimy refuse filled with tuberculosis, typhoid fever, and other germs. Children stood "half-buried in piles of filth and rubbish, their merry whoops" signaling "that they were having the time of their lives." The columnist observed: "Not all children are Negroes, Mexicans, or half-breeds. Nearly a dozen white children, whose pinched, little faces showed plainly the terrible poverty that was their lot." Engulfing those who trolled for its singular riches, the dump's rancid blanket of unbearable stench overrode all. Mattie De Turk, formerly America's Parachute Queen, Miss Hazel Keyes reigned over the entire putrid realm.[119]

Early on a June 1904 evening, one of her dump's always-burning, paper-fueled fires raged out of control. Ferocious flames lapped dangerously near the De Turk house as the family battled its blistering heat.

At that moment, two drunken Los Angeles Rubbish Company workers arrived. Rolling atop their wagon past the large entrance gates, Walter Langley and J.W. Blackmar stopped next to the out-of-control fire. In their inebriated state, the men began pitching their load of scrap paper and other trash onto the fire. When the De Turks protested, one of the intruders drew a knife and threatened to slice Mattie's throat. Her son entered the dispute, and the other man leveled a revolver at him, chasing him straight through the fire. The family night of terror finally ended with the arrest of Langley and Blackmar on a charge of assault with a deadly weapon.[120]

Farmer John's Vernon meat-processing plant stands near the former De Turk ranch site in 2021. With no park or school in Vernon, industry dominates the area around the De Turk's former property. (Gail Kalt Collection)

Los Angeles' "Prolific Producer of Disease"

Labeling them the city's "prolific producer of disease," an editorial writer maintained that Vernon hog operations threatened broader Los Angeles. Including the De Turk's acreage, dumps covered 80 total acres in Vernon by 1906. Much of the city's garbage "finds its way into prosperous homes in the guise of breakfast bacon and sugar-cured hams," wrote the editor. "It is a somewhat dubious fact that much of the pork we eat is the product not of the soil, but the swill of local groceries, restaurants, and green goods shops." Each day, "hog raisers cart away great quantities of the refuse to feed to their hogs," and inspectors trace meat condemned as "unfit for food" back to the garbage dump. "It is these same swill-fed hogs that cause most of the troubles arising from meat. Their flesh is soft, and they are easy prey for hog cholera and other diseases."

Testimony demonstrated that swine death from hog cholera "makes little difference to the raiser." Several local hog ranchers continued to vend the rank product "to some peddler, who dresses the meat and, in turn, sells it to restaurants and butcher shops, or kills the hog himself and sells it surreptitiously." The editor provided a description fit to turn stomachs: "Floating over the neighborhood in odiferous waves of concentrated rottenness, the gases are said to have caused much sickness. Dark clouds of effluvia poison" the Vernon air. The odor grows "unbearable [at night]; when the sickly pall of the clammy vapor settles like a shroud on the dwellings. The smell floats for miles over Los Angeles." (Los Angeles Herald, *June 24, 1906, "Babies Devour Garbage;"* Los Angeles Times, *January 27, 1906, "Awful Odor Over Vernon."*)

Wagons, buggies, and streetcars rolled past the hotels Lexington and Rosslyn and the Barker Bros. building on the left side of Los Angeles' Main Street ca. 1906. Few Angelinos caught the drift of Vernon's horrible conditions or the process that readied pork for their dining tables. (USCL, CHS-5088, https:// doi.org/10.25549/chs-m8109)

17

Fire, A Grisly Find, & Beatin' Back the Bully

Martha "Mattie" De Turk, née Miss Hazel Keyes' propensity for making news continued as the first decade of the 1900s unfolded. With traffic brisk at the sandpit and the porky crew gobbling, Mattie found herself involved in "one of the greatest" Southern California murder mysteries. The tale commenced in 1906 when Mattie visited her cousin Mary Chapman, Thomas "Posey Tulare" Horton's sister. That August, Posey drove his wagon to Ocean Park, California, where Mary managed the Horton family's two rooming-house hotels to pick up Mattie and take her back to Vernon. With Mattie aboard, Posey ran his team up into Temescal Canyon's "Dead Horse" Gulch, searching for water for his horses and a place to eat lunch. Known as a favorite spot for dumping equine carcasses, the location proved a sour choice for picnicking. The awful stench that only dead flesh renders swallowed Posey and Mattie as they stepped down from the wagon. Almost overcome, Mattie noticed a piece of red silk in the underbrush. Nearby, the rotting remains of a frail, well-dressed woman shocked the bestunken pair. A button-down blouse and silk skirt draped loosely over the desiccated remains.[121]

Mattie and Posey first notified road graders working on the Malibu railroad, who reported their discovery to authorities in Santa Monica.

Hearing the dreadful news, Posey's sister, Mary Chapman, rushed into Guidinger's undertaking house to view the remains. Infused with a "haunting fear" for one of her roomers, she scanned the grizzled human carcass for signs of a blonde-haired, married young woman who "fell out" with her husband and disappeared about three weeks earlier. Relief showered Chapman when she noticed strands of the victim's black hair. Suspicion of murder surrounded Posey and his brother "Hemp" Horton, running to the notion that the corpse belonged to Hemp's fiancée, Clara Armstrong. Said by her brother to have "decamped" Santa Barbara to marry Hemp two months earlier, Clara vanished. Posey's circumstances darkened when he disappeared after issuing a full report to law officers.[122]

A Los Angeles Times artist rendered this illustration of murder victim Claddie Besold, whose body Mattie and her cousin Posey found in 1906. (Los Angeles Times, *September 21, 1906.*)

Facts soon exonerated both Horton brothers when identification of the remains pinpointed Claddie Besold as the victim. Diminutive Deputy Sheriff Charles Gilbert's fine detective work led to a second-degree murder conviction of Claddie's husband, Bavarian butcher Anton Orter Besold. Testimony showed that the meatcutter, beset by the burden of his wife's wasting away from tuberculosis, fired a fatal 38-caliber slug that earned him life in prison. Evidence of Besold's serial polygamy added further intrigue to the case, which fascinated Angelinos.[123]

Women Who Claim to Have Been Wooed
and Wedded by the Butcher

BESOLD'S MATRIMONIAL PLUNGES
Married Claddie Alderman, Fort Brady, Mich., August, 1901.
Married Claddie Besold, Caspar, Wyo., October 17, 1903.
Proposed to Bellingham Bay woman, 1904.
Married Mrs. Martha D. Picket, at Santa Ana, August 21, '06.
Proposed to Washington woman six weeks ago, but was arrested the day before his proposed marriage.

Los Angeles Herald, November 6, 1906

Tennessee-born brothers William and Orrin Horton would come to control 1,600 acres in and near Calabasas, California. Miss Hazel and Orrin's son, Posey "Tulare" Horton, remained close for decades. Posey, who lost his wife and young daughter to spinal meningitis, lived on the family's acreage west of Calabasas by 1906. The town's only storekeeper, he also owned Calabasas' wild, rundown cantina. A Los Angeles Times *story explained that he oversaw "a tottering collection of shabby, slab-sided, white-washed adobes [that] squat under the shade of a few disreputable-looking trees, nearly all the windows have been cracked, knocked out or shot out. Old rags have been stuffed into some of the cracks." His cantina stood as "the place in prohibition Calabasas where everyone gets drunk on Saturday night. Where Mexican* cholos *and whites, both men and women, pound the loose boards of the dingy hall in wild, hilarious dances until the Sabbath dawn pales through the broken panes of the smoky, unwashed windows." (*Los Angeles Times, *September 9, 1906, "Mystery of Temescal Deepens: Posey Horton Tells His Story.")*

Safely back home in Vernon, Mattie resumed her managerial role at the family's ranch. A wellspring of newspaper items, she next wrangled with Vernon Trustee William M. Stephens. Their long-running feud first arose after the City of Vernon incorporated as California's solely "industrial" city in 1905. Boundary changes left Mattie's huge garbage heap divided between Los Angeles and the new town. When Vernon's leaders objected to wagons depositing refuse in their portion, it forced Mattie to direct her drivers to dump rubbish only on the Los Angeles side.[124]

Los Angeles Herald, May 18, 1894

Insisting she stood in compliance with the order, Mattie maintained that Vernon's trustees ran a "campaign of persecution" against her. She declared that Trustee Stephens, a fellow hog farmer, rode the hardest due to a "personal grudge against her." Stephens' land abutted hers, and Mattie claimed that he instructed a friend "who is in league with him, to go to his [Stephens'] property and dare me to go with him. He hoped to arrest me in Vernon, where I would certainly have been convinced [convicted]." After Stephens ordered two of Mattie's drivers arrested, the pair insisted that men kidnapped and dragged them to the Vernon side. When Mattie confronted her nemesis, she stated, "He pulled off his coat and wanted me to fight. Now, he weighs over 220 pounds, and I only weigh 130, and I am nearly fifty years old. I'm no prizefighter, and I told him it was the first time I had ever heard of a big man like him challenging a small woman. He had to go away without fighting."[125]

The brouhaha peaked in December 1907 as Mattie drove through Vernon with a friend. Approaching in a heavy wagon, Stephens forced her to drive "far out of the roadway, out of pure malice" and ordered her "to keep off the road while he was using it." Mattie reported his spiteful antics to two health officers who helped her file a complaint against Stephens. The Los Angeles City Prosecutor arrested Vernon's bully, charging him with disturbing the peace, but its Police Court acquitted and released him. Back and forth flew the tit-for-tat as Stephens retaliated by causing the arrest of Mattie's son Eddie on a minor theft charge. Eddie filed suit after his acquittal, accusing his tormenter of false imprisonment, but he vanished the night before his scheduled testimony against Stephens.[126]

Mrs. M. H. de Turk,

Martha H. De Turk

Los Angeles Times, June 22, 1914

18

Trouble in Paradise

Mattie feared the worst when her son Eddie disappeared before his scheduled court appearance. Believing "men who laid in wait" snatched him, she stated, "The boy disappeared as though swallowed up by the ground. There are acres of land covered by piles of rubbish on my property. If Edward is not found soon, I shall put men to work to search for his body in these rubbish heaps." She added that he took her purse when he left. "Two days after he disappeared, one of the dogs brought the purse to the house," explained his heartsick mother. "It was covered with the dirt from one of the rubbish heaps." Quelling her angst, Mattie's wayward son reappeared to continue along his agonizing trail.[127]

Edward S. "Eddie" Keyes found no easy row to hoe. Born in October 1889 in a boxcar in the Oregon woods, he suffered convulsions for his first three months. Problems compounded when he and his mother attended a picnic at Agua Caliente, Arizona. About 14 at the time, Eddie joined in the day's *Corrido de Gallo*, or "rooster pull," racing across the arena and leaning down to grab the head of a rooster buried to its neck in the sand. Losing his balance, he crashed to the ground, hit his head on a pile of rocks, and ruptured an intestine. Unconscious for 24 hours and rushed to Los Angeles for treatment, he escaped the hospital right before surgery to repair his intestinal tear and slipped into ruin.[128]

Fleeing to Chicago, Eddie "preferred the company of dogs to [that] of human beings," explained a *Santa Ana Register* report. "He lived dirty and ragged. His mother learned that he had been drinking whiskey in the riverbed and slipped into his mother's kitchen at night for food. He was operated upon for the rupture [and] again ran away to Chicago. He lived with tramps, and his habits became bestial in the extreme. Through drink, he sank lower and lower." Eddie also lived in a Jawbone Canyon cave, 120 miles north of his Vernon home. He shared the cavern with a pet snake owned by ex-cavalryman Edward "Red" Schaefer. Though she acknowledged his crushing injury left Eddie with "the mind of a five-year-old," Mattie's motherly love ran deep. To her utmost chagrin, liquor's stranglehold helped propel the young man to serial pedophilia and unthinkably vicious murder. In a sad reality, two of her three precious sons trampled over both Mattie and the law across decades. The reasons for the family's extreme dysfunction might lie in the boys' involvement with their mother's "circus-atmosphere" lifestyle during her parachuting days and frequent moving from one performance to another. Their parents' violent relationship, combative approach to life, and criminal behaviors also undoubtedly influenced their behavior as adults.[129]

Mattie and Joshua De Turk shared an almost three-decade age disparity, and marital feathers flew in 1911. When the Mr., now 74, told Mattie he planned to sell all the couple's hogs because they didn't "have a nickel," his disclosure stunned her. "We had $11,000 saved up, and one day my husband told me we were broke," she later testified in court. "I was amazed." She declared that businessman C.B. "Habeas Corpus" Ladd then "came with a patent [on a digging machine used in mining] and wanted my husband to put up the money to get it going. They conversed in front of our little home by the honeysuckles. Mr. Ladd told him it would be worth millions. If my husband went into it, he said, we would be riding in our private [railroad] car."[130]

J.G. held off investing at the time but soon told his wife he'd "gone in on the patent." Mattie protested when Ladd appeared at their home wanting $375, but J.G. assured her the venture would "make us money." She later explained: "The $11,000 was gone; he had put the money into the digger" for Ladd's mining operation. "He told me a great foundry would be built on our ranch, and it spelled wealth for us. He said we must mortgage our home for $4,500 and asked me to sign the mortgage."[131]

With her usual resolve, Los Angeles' Sand-Lot Queen refused her husband's demands to sign the mortgage document. J.G. shouted, "Mattie, you must sign," and grabbed her by the throat. Promoter Ladd yelled, "Make her sign it: don't turn her loose." Later, while giving courtroom testimony, Mattie leaped to her feet at the witness stand with fists clenched to illustrate. Following the judge's admonishment to calm down, Mattie stated: "I started to run away, and Mr. Ladd grabbed me by the shoulder, shouting, 'No, you won't. Make her sign it—don't let her go.'" Joshua De Turk told his wife, "We are ruined if you don't sign this mortgage." The tough-minded businesswoman remained steadfast, withholding her consent. A neighbor attested, "I asked her, 'Did you give him [Ladd] a good one?'" Mattie responded, "You bet I did. I beat him with my umbrella. I kicked his wig off and gave him thunder. I said I wouldn't sign the mortgage if he killed me." When her husband later apologized, she offered, "Let us get on our knees and pray," and Joshua replied, "I don't believe in prayers." She told the court, "He asked me not to speak of it, and I never told a living soul."[132]

Complications flooded Mattie's life as word of the De Turk hog, sand, and tin can triumph spread. A March 1909 *Los Angeles Times* article entitled "Wins Wealth from Rubbish" fueled an already excited crowd wanting to take advantage of her prosperity. The account deemed the De Turk enterprise a "Real Gold Mine," stating, "No sooner did the facts become known that the wasteland the De Turks had bought was

Los Angeles Times, March 21, 1909

fairly coining them money that many began looking with envious eyes. Lust-filled real estate salesmen vowed they would cloud her title. On every side, attempts were made to secure her title, by hook or by crook. Offers were made to purchase it, threats of condemnation followed [and] in spite of the pressure, she remained firm in her determination to retain her hold on the sand pits."[133]

Vernon operations fed 12,000 hogs on organic and semi-organic discards by October 1909. However, the porkers failed to keep pace with the ever-building mountain of garbage. Despite the couple's profitable sand and can enterprise, their swine business continued to help foul the Southern California air, bringing recrimination. N.L. Blabon, Ward Six Central Improvement District president, declared, "The nuisance at Vernon was bad enough when only one-third of the city's garbage was being dumped there. Imagine what it is now, in hot weather, when all the refuse of the city is dumped there." Blabon declared the problem "a menace to health, an insult to our self-respect, and, is bound in time, to stop all progress in our section of the community." He demanded the board take immediate action to clean up the horrid Vernon hog compound and its pong, declaring, "There is no question in my mind that serious epidemic problems may arise if the city continues to dump its garbage in the sun."[134]

Trash problems paled, however, when Mattie's son, Joseph A. Keyes, added havoc and pain to his mother's life. Working as a glazier in San Francisco, Joseph visited Mattie at her Vernon home in November 1909. While there, he watched her hide money to purchase an automobile as a Christmas present for his brother Eddie. Ignoring the proverb regarding stealing from one's mother, Joseph absconded with $580 of her $740 savings.[135]

'BLACK HAND' IN CRIME MYSTERY

Los Angeles Herald, February 24, 1919

Tension compounded when Mattie received a shadowy Black Hand extortion letter in January 1910. The message demanded she put $1,000 under a designated pile of trash or risk Joseph's murder. More letters arrived, along with threatening telephone calls. One promised to annihilate the whole family and demolish the De Turk homestead if Mattie failed to make a $100,000 payment. She rushed to Los Angeles County Sheriff W.A. Hammel, who swore in Daniel Todd, the night watchman at Mattie's dump, as a Special Deputy. A later account announced, "The watchman proved true to his trust, and the letters and calls ceased." Despite the rosy report, danger loitered.[136]

Investigation revealed a motive for Joseph's theft from Mattie and the Black Hand letters she received. Los Angeles Deputy Sheriff Claude Mathewson tracked Joseph to San Francisco's 1157 Octavia St., where he lived as "man and wife" with Mrs. Nora Mack, alias Miss Kittie McVay. In fact, Miss Kittie's real husband, Charles Mack, stood as one of San Francisco's most notorious, corrupt, and violent desperados of the early 20th century. Mack, alias the "Buff Kid," ruled "The Buff Kid Gang," thugs above little and beyond nothing in their pursuit of money and other spoils. No one's idea of a good boy, this nasty scoundrel's brutality defined him, and, convicted of theft of $100 in gold from a Fruitvale woman, he sat in San Quentin State Prison. Now, Mattie's son Joseph lived with the brute's wife under matrimonial pretense.

Joseph Keyes had stumbled into a welter of Bay Area violence, intimidation, and retribution. A purse-plundering petty criminal, he found a more cruel and vicious world when he moved in with the Buff Kid's spouse. One might easily imagine the Kid's level of appreciation for Joseph's living with his wife while he slept behind bars.

San Quentin prison photo of Charles Mack, alias The Buff Kid. His right eye appears to show the damage inflicted when an attacker cut his face with a knife. (San Francisco Examiner, *May 8, 1909, "Plot Revealed to Kidnap Her Child."*)

Unwilling to let "boys be boys," Mattie pressed theft charges against her wayward son. In addition, authorities arrested Joseph and two other hoodlums for stealing 2,000 cigars from Herman Kaiser's cigar store on Golden Gate Avenue. When Joseph went to trial, she testified that her boy rode under the "evil influence" of the unsavory Nora Mack. "My son is not a bad boy," declared Mattie. "This woman, my son advises me, has a number of boys his own age who will commit any crime she suggests, that she may wear fine clothes and live well," declared Mattie.

She begged the court to send Joseph to prison to protect him from the Buff Kid Gang and free him from the wicked woman's grasp. There, or to the Panama Canal Zone, where his brothers Edward and Henry worked. "If you send my boy to Panama," the mother implored his honor, "I will compel him to send you $5 a month for five years to be handed as a donation to a charitable institution for the injury he has done to the community." The judge declined the offer of money but directed a detective to escort Joseph to the dock and ensure he stepped "aboard the steamer leaving for Panama" and set the police on the trail of Nora Mack for vagrancy.[137]

The Buff Kid Welcomes Mattie's Boy
to the Bottom of the Barrel

Buff Kid's criminal life might have served as resource material for a "tough guy" role in 1930s movies such as *The Public Enemy* and *Angels with Dirty Faces*. The tale reads like a polished script, from the strategies employed on both sides of the law to the language used.

Arrested several times as a "bunco steerer" (swindler, cheat) but never convicted, Charles Mack ran under the name "Buff Kid." In 1902, authorities forced him out of San Francisco after he attacked would-be attorney "Curley" Riley. When his brother, F.A. Mack, faced robbery charges, the Kid gave Riley $50 to defend him and left town. After Riley wasted the money and his brother caught 20 years in San Quentin State Prison, the Kid went looking for Riley with a club, but Curley slashed him across the face with a razor. The slice rendered Mack easily identifiable to law enforcement, and the "hard character" roamed from San Francisco to Sacramento as a petty thief, pickpocket, and scammer.

Near the end of 1905, the Buff Kid and Charles Craig led a vicious Christmas morning beating of two Sacramento policemen at the city's Art Saloon & Dance Hall. "Set upon by a gang of toughs" while trying to "quell a row," Sergeant John A. Wilson and Officer Arthur Ryan incurred a nasty pummeling. Wilson lay in the street "knocked unconscious by his own club" and later reported that not a single barkeeper stepped in to help him. Other thugs delivered Ryan a vicious thrashing. Treated like royalty while jailed, Mack and his accomplice received visits from "their women friends and [were] served with the finest meals from the outside."

The notorious Buff Kid served less than four years in San Quentin State Prison for his lead role in the lawmen's assault. Continuing his criminal life, the Kid drugged a Fruitvale, California woman, Edith McCrea, and stole $110 in gold from her purse. He and his minions then tried to poison her with morphine-tainted whiskey and threatened to kidnap her daughter to prevent her from testifying. Convicted of grand larceny, he returned to San Quentin, leaving Miss Kittie McVay to perpetrate her scams in San Francisco. In the penitentiary, the Kid's efforts turned to threatening Mattie De Turk after her son Joseph moved in with his wife following his incarceration. (*Sacramento Bee*, December 30, 1905, "Is the Art Dive to Win Out Again?"; *The Morning Call*, [San Francisco], May 23, 1911, "Marriage License Recalls Scandal.")

"The purpose of life is not to be happy. It is to be useful, to be honorable, to be compassionate, to have it make some difference that you have lived and lived well." Ralph Waldo Emerson

*Bamboozled out of $110 by the Buff Kid in Oakland's notorious Press Saloon, a "rendezvous of known thieves" and "a resort of fallen women," Edith McCrea held a reputation as an alcoholic. Her husband blamed her for the "ultra-sensational" incident and pummeled her repeatedly afterward. (*Oakland Tribune, *May 19, 1909, "Mrs. McCrea Plans to Flee the City"; May 17, 1909, "Woman Beaten by Husband Until She Is Black and Blue.")*

Shock and horror stalked the corner of Vernon, California's Santa Fe Avenue, and George Street on February 22, 1910. That day, Mattie's son, Eddie, reportedly loaded with liquor, began harassing his step-father Joshua De Turk for money to go to town. The dispute escalated when Mattie whacked Eddie over the head with a pitchfork handle, and he began brandishing a revolver. "When I found he had a gun,

I told him to give it to me," she later explained. "When he did not, I started to take it away from him."

Talking with Joshua nearby, Special Deputy Daniel Todd rushed to help Mattie. Eddie "handed me the gun, and I grabbed it by the muzzle," she declared. "The next thing I knew, I heard a shot fired, and the pistol went flying in the air. When I found Mr. Todd shot, I didn't know what to do. I screamed for help and stooped over the dead body." The worst came when Eddie, unaware he had killed Todd, pled, "Don't do that, Dan, you'll scare mamma." Falling to the ground sobbing, Eddie knelt over his older friend's corpse. "He started to hunt for the gun, saying he was going to blow his brains out," Mattie continued. "I told him not to do that; that I would say I killed him [Todd] and I would go to jail. I said, 'If you're going to kill yourself, you kill me too, because I can't live without you, Eddie.'" Under-Sheriff Robert T. Brain soon arrived and took Mattie and her son to jail.[138]

When questioned, Eddie remained silent about Todd's killing and feigned a laugh of bravado that fooled no one. "A nervous twitching of the corners of the mouth showed

ACCIDENT OR MURDER?

KILLS MAN HE SAYS HE WOULD "GO TO HELL FOR."

City Watchman Shot Through the Heart by Youth During Struggle for Revolver Started by Boy's Mother—Both Are in Jail and Son, After Show of Bravery, Breaks Down and Weeps.

Los Angeles Times, February 23, 1910

plainly the deep emotion with which he was struggling," claimed one account. Thrusting forward "a pair of brawny arms to the officer" taking his deposition, Eddie declared, "Yes, I am tattooed on both arms," before breaking down and crying. Eddie sobbed, "Todd is dead. He's been killed—he was just like a brother to me—he belonged to the same Eagles lodge—he would have given me anything in the world." Then, issuing a mournful cry, he declared, "I'd go to hell for him."[139]

The report stated, "Authorities do not give Keys [sic] an entirely good name. They say he had been drinking at the time and do not speak well of his ambitions to make his way in the world." Eddie, "for

Edward S. Keyes
Los Angeles Herald, February 23, 1910

all he has attained [of] man's estate—so far as age is concerned, is but a puny boy and far under the average height. He is a pretty solid specimen of little manhood, nevertheless, well-developed muscularly and weighs a good deal more than would be guessed by his appearance." Though he sported "two rows of faultless teeth, his face is not prepossessing, [unattractive] indicating an intelligence rather below average."[140]

Justice rode on whether Edward S. Keyes murdered Special Deputy Daniel Todd or if he died by accidental shooting. A coroner's jury issued an "accidental death" verdict, but the District Attorney's office charged Eddie with Todd's murder. The judge set bail at $10,000, and Mattie's soul brimmed with anguish as love for her son and torment over his actions dueled with her respect and affection for her long-time friend Todd.

Mattie sat in the courtroom draped in black

mourning attire for Eddie's preliminary hearing. Her attorney escorted the heart-stricken woman to the witness stand, where she broke down in tears. Eddie's attorney moved to lower his bond to $5,000 because "the boy's mother had had several attacks of heart failure since" his incarceration. Mattie's appeal drew victory, and the judge lowered Eddie's bond, Mattie paid it, and the court released him.[141]

Joshua De Turk took the witness chair when the case came to trial. He swore that Eddie and his mother suffered frequent arguments, adding that Mattie often "upbraided the son for wasting his time and money on the society of lewd women." Deputy Todd "always seemed to take a great interest in the boy [Edward]," declared J.G. "Many a time, he said he was going to make a man out of him." Disputing police reports, he added that "Eddie was sober at the time." The young man's attorney issued an inspiring plea for dismissal. "Before he concluded, there was hardly a dry eye in the courtroom," noted a reporter. Following a brief deliberation, the judge cast Edward S. Keyes' murder charge aside. The tragic killing of Daniel Todd proved just one more astonishing incident in the incredible, textured life of America's early parachute superstar and Los Angeles' fierce Sand-Lot Queen.

Heartbreak delivered Mattie another vicious blow the following November when her son Joseph, 23, met a brutal death in Sacramento. After returning from his 1910 exile to Panama, Joseph, using the last name Romig, moved to Sacramento in May 1911 and took work as a glazier for Capital Paint Company. Around 6:00 p.m. on

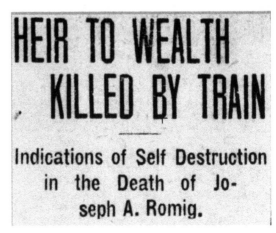

Sacramento Daily Union, November 6, 1911

HEIR TO WEALTH KILLED BY TRAIN

Indications of Self Destruction in the Death of Joseph A. Romig.

November 5, 1911, a yard watchman for the Southern Pacific Railroad, L.H. Wilson, encountered a man walking near the tracks. When asked if he held a pass allowing him to enter the property, the man scurried away behind a row of railcars. Later that evening, as he walked between the railcars to uncouple them, yard crew foreman William Norton tripped over Joseph's dead body near the spot where watchman Wilson had last seen the fleeing man. Evidence revealed that the bolts on one of the cars' bolster had crashed down upon Joseph, breaking his neck, back, and shoulder and killing him instantly. Coroner W.F. Gormley's inquest failed to expose a reason for Joseph's hideous death. However, the *Sacramento Record-Union* reporter declared, "How he came to be under the wheels, unless intentionally, is a mystery," adding that "indications of self-destruction" existed.[142]

National Home for Disabled Volunteer Soldiers, Pacific Branch, Domiciliary No. 6, Wilshire & Sawtelle Boulevards, Los Angeles, Los Angeles County, CA (https://www.loc.gov/pictures/item/ca0253.photos.011990p)

Henry Keyes Makes the Grade

While her sons Joseph and Eddie played loose with legality and civility, eldest son Henry C. Keyes found a good measure of success. Henry enlisted in the U. S. Army at Pendleton, Oregon, on September 2, 1899, after the Battle of Manila ignited the Filipino-American War that February. He joined the 39th Regiment Volunteer Infantry's I Company stationed at Tanauan in Batangas Province. Two months after his arrival, the conflict intensified as Philippine independence fighters adopted guerrilla-style combat.

Despite contracting malaria at some point during 1900, Private Keyes served 19 months in the humid Philippine jungles until his muster out in May 1901. The 5' 7" Portland native fought the vicious disease for the next three years before entering the Pacific Branch of the National Homes for Disabled Volunteer Soldiers at Sawtelle in late August 1904. Suffering from dysentery as well as malaria by then, Henry remained under care until his discharge the following June. He listed Mattie De Turk as his nearest kin and his occupation as cook and butcher.

Henry's initial marriage, in 1898, appeared to end when he set sail for the Panama Canal Zone in late January 1909. That October, the court granted the couple a divorce in Los Angeles. First employed as a steward in the Subsistence Department for $60 per month, he worked as a department inspector by August 1913. Henry earned $150 plus a living allowance each month before his March 1915 resignation and return from Cristóbal Colón, Panama, to New Orleans aboard the United Fruit Company's "Great White Fleet" ship, the *Turrialba*.

Henry ran a hotel in Oatman, Arizona, in 1917 with his partner, William B. Gilbert, a water company civil engineer. Gilbert also worked as a cook in a restaurant along the Mohave County Road. That year, Henry wed 24-year-old North Dakota divorcée Cassie May Langdon. This union produced a son in 1922 and a daughter in 1924. By 1930, the couple owned a home on Kingman, Arizona's Front Street (renamed Andy Devine Avenue) valued at $12,000 ($202,125 in 2021), and Henry toiled as a machinist working on mining machinery. Henry C. Keyes died on July 11, 1937, in Los Angeles. Honored for his military service, he lies buried in the Los Angeles National Cemetery. Cassie May Keyes later served as the informant on the death certificate of her mother-in-law, Mattie De Turk. *(Twelfth Census of the United States, Schedule No. 1.—Population, Military, and Naval Population, Company I, 39th Regiment Infantry, U.S. Army—Philippine Islands Tanauan, Batangas Province, 270; U.S. National Homes for Disabled Volunteer Soldiers, #6697, discharged June 1, 1905; U.S. Panama Canal Zone Service Lists, Service Record Cards, 1904–1920, #1238)*

19

"Patrolling the Grounds Like an Armed Sentry" & Shotgun Showdown

Mattie De Turk grabbed headlines again in 1911. The tumult started when the City of Los Angeles purchased ground for dumping its ever-growing mountain of garbage. Henceforth, drivers had to run their horse-drawn wagons across about 400 yards of the De Turk property to dump their loads. Unimpressed by the plan, Mattie defended her land with customary vigor.

Early one November morning, about 10 trash wagons made it through and deposited their loads before she arrived to intervene. As teamster J. S. Sanders drove his rig under the nearby Santa Fe Railroad Bridge, she yelled out, cautioning him not to encroach. Within minutes,

Mattie De Turk (inset) stands next to one of the city's garbage wagons in this Los Angeles Times *artist's drawing. (*Los Angeles Times, *March 9, 1913)*

scores of other drivers arrived to find their access to the city dump blocked. "With a determination that an auto load of police, the board of public works, and scores of teamsters could not break, Mrs. J. G. De Turk of Vernon stood guard over a narrow strip of land leading to the garbage dumping ground and personally prevented trespassing," read the *Los Angeles Times* tale. "As a result, over 75 loaded garbage trucks are now standing at Edwin and Harriet streets." The report explained, "The men at first stormed, but the little woman, garbed in a hunting coat, red skirt, and sailor hat, broke their arguments with soft-toned reason until the men changed their tone." Ready for "a bloody battle," several "blue-coated officers" arrived. However, "working-class sensibilities" prevailed, and the officers witnessed "a party of good-natured equally even-tempered woman." Inspector Humphries of the Board of Public Works arrived and demanded, "Where is the man who says he owns this land?" Mattie answered in a soft voice, "I am the 'man' who owns this property." Pausing to confer with the police and drivers, the inspector soon retreated to his vehicle and departed.[143]

Mattie explained that the city had "forcibly prevented" her from getting garbage to feed 1,500 starving hogs several years earlier. "Another time, the city would have allowed an oil company to lay a pipeline across my property," she continued. "That time, I took the same stand I did here and won. Each time I fought my own battles and won them. The City of Los Angeles will have to dump its garbage elsewhere or build a bridge to the dumping ground." The incident cost about 17 hours of lost garbage collection time before the Board of Public Works withdrew all the city wagons, sending them back to using old city dumpsites.[144]

Acquitted in 1910 on the charge of murdering his friend, Special Deputy Daniel Todd, Mattie's youngest boy proved his dissolute nature two years later. In February 1912, Eddie accosted a 10-year-old newsboy at Los Angeles' Seventh and San Pedro Streets. He committed sexual atrocities before slashing the child with a butcher knife and leaving him for dead. When the youth recovered, he picked Eddie out of a lineup, and the judge sentenced him to seven years at San Quentin for committing "abominable statutory relations." As Eddie left the courtroom, Mattie issued a resounding wail, fainted, and tumbled onto the floor. Taken to the city's Receiving Hospital, she suffered a severe bruise on her face.[145]

Things took another downturn in the De Turk home when Joshua signed an accord with contractor N.O. Harmon for hauling sand off their property for a small amount per load on May 2, 1914. Two weeks passed before Mattie caught wind of the agreement. Livid, she believed Harmon represented some corporation bent on usurping her profits. Pocket-sized Mattie De Turk stood her ground again four miles southeast of downtown Los Angeles. Enraged when Mattie challenged his pact with Harmon, J. G. assaulted his wife on May 16, 1914, shattering the last semblance of their relationship. Mattie met the octogenarian's attack with fierce resistance, and he backed off. Though they continued to live in the house, the couple had nothing to do with each other. Mattie ordered a wooden fence with locking gates built around her sand and gravel operation, and workers chained the gates. After gaining surreptitious access, contractor Harmon began measuring the area for his planned operation. Mattie burst upon him with her large gun and demanded his exit. Deeming it a "sensational ejectment," the *Times* reported that, since that moment, "she patrolled the grounds armed like a sentry." Mattie soon appeared before a judge to show cause why she shouldn't honor the contract her husband signed.[146]

Violence and stark terror revisited Mattie in June 1914. Her legal and marital miseries set aside for the moment; she dressed for an evening at the theater in her bedroom at the Vernon home. As she bent to pick up a pair of shoes, the booming report of a shotgun announced a hail of buckshot exploding through her window. The Sand-Lot Queen dropped to her knees to hide behind her sewing machine as pellets ripped into the mannequin she used as a dress form. To its tender target's good fortune, the firearm's errant blast forced her window shade up, throwing light on the spot where two unknown men lurked. Both light-bathed criminals raced away into the darkness, but not before Mattie and her friend and family cook, Mrs. Birtha Williams, hurried

This photo captured Mattie De Turk's resolve as she stood beside her son Edward S. Keyes when she stopped 75 loaded garbage wagons from crossing her property in November 1911. (Los Angeles Herald, *November 25, 1911*)

Hears Bullets Whistle Through Her Hat

Mrs. Mattie de Turk,

Los Angeles Times, June 19, 1914

to the window and caught a clear look at one of them. Unscathed by the attack, Mattie declared that she "owes her life to the fact that the shot caused the window shade to fly up" and "undoubtedly prevented a second, fatal shot."[147]

This latest episode overwhelmed the rock-tough little woman, who soon rested in a hospital suffering from shock. Adding to the nightmare of her narrow escape from death, Mattie's elderly husband paid no attention to the shotgun blast and chose not to investigate her attempted murder. Furious with him, Mattie returned from the hospital to find that friends had double barricaded her house to protect her. Sheriff's officers defended the home's perimeter while workers moved Mattie's bed into the middle of the house for further protection. She insisted that her property's treasured sand provided the motive for her attempted killing. When Joshua De Turk finally spoke to Mattie four days after the shooting, he demanded that she take the lock off the gate barring Harmon's entry. Mattie later swore that he added, "I wish you were dead and out of my way; you interfere with my business and keep me from making money." America's former sky sensation shared her tale of losing the sand and gravel pits in court: "My husband signed the contract to sell our land without even reading it over properly prior. Because I will not stand quietly by and see our years of work taken away from us, I am made a target." Ever a battler, Mattie continued, "With me out of the way, those who want our land would not have any trouble wresting it from Mr. De Turk."[148]

A *Times* story that September exposed the secret of Mattie's earlier persona, well-kept for more than a decade. The newspaper divulged that Mrs. Martha H. de Turk, the Sand-Lot Queen, stood "revealed in a more romantic character. For years she has been the wife of Joshua de Turk without suspicion that she and Hazel Keyes, 'Queen of the Balloon,' are one and the same." Citing Miss Hazel's ability to electrify "thousands by her balloon ascensions in this city," the story recounted her days with Miss Jennie Yan Yan. "A favorite feat was to release a monkey on a parachute from a great height." Following her spine-tingling sky career, "She dropped out of sight." Though Mattie challenged his statement, her husband claimed she waited years to "lay bare her identity to him as the famous balloonist."[149]

Joshua De Turk, described as "patriarchal in appearance," asserted his right in court to unilaterally sign a contract with sand and gravel contractor N.O. Harmon. The elderly Vernon Hog King declared he bought the 14-acre property before meeting and marrying Mattie. In fact, J.G. had owned the land since at least December 1891, when he granted the Vernon Irrigation Co. right-of-way across the tract. That she contributed to the maintenance and improvement of the property and superintended the couple's lucrative business interests also stood clear. Nevertheless, the court awarded Harmon a perpetual injunction barring Mattie from interfering with his removing sand and gravel from the property. The *Times* prematurely reported, "Mrs. De Turk allowed the suit to go by default."[150]

Miss Hazel Keyes hid her high-flying identity for more than a decade after moving to Los Angeles in about 1903. (Oregon Historical Society A-886)

20

Divorce, Death, & Devastation

Martha H. and Joshua G. de Turk each claimed adultery and cruelty when they sued each other for divorce in 1914. Because it involved a large amount of property and would "develop no end of very sensational testimony," the case demanded utmost privacy amid burning societal interest. County deputy sheriffs rotated duty each day to safeguard all evidence from the press. With the public hungering for the scandalous details of the juicy proceedings, the *Los Angeles Times* boasted an inside source and distributed "the essentials of the case to readers daily." The insider reported Mattie's claim that the couple "never had a cross word until four years ago." Her lawyer asked, "Who caused the trouble?"[151]

"This man named 'Habeas Corpus Ladd,'" she replied, recounting how Ladd and her husband battled her for money to finance the digging machine for mining. Mattie told the courtroom a tale that sounded "like the plaint of a galley slave," full of "undreamed of hardships." She testified that, despite their reported immense wealth, her husband never bought her a single article of clothing. Further, she picked their vegetables from the dump's condemned foods and canned goods. Mattie added that she collected Joshua's underwear and socks from the dump and mended them. Joshua never took her to one show or other entertainment and brought her a present only one time, when

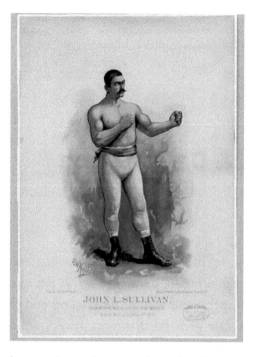

JOHN L. SULLIVAN.

Deemed "the last of the bare-knuckle champions who pounded each other without gloves for hours in marathon matches that lasted for as many as 75 rounds," John L. Sullivan lost the heavyweight championship in 21 rounds to "Gentleman Jim" Corbett on September 7, 1892. The bout proved "a watershed for professional boxing as the sport moved out of the shadows of criminality into the realm of public entertainment." (hdl.loc. gov/loc.pnp/pga.05673)

he gave her a free sample pack of candy from a grocery store. She made money selling photos of boxing's iconic "Gentleman Jim" Corbett vs. John L. Sullivan 1892 thriller, which she hid in an empty oil can under the house for her needs. "It was my own," she stated. "I earned it. It was mine to do with as I pleased. I kept it there so the members of my family wouldn't know anything about it." In early October 1914, Los Angeles County Superior Court made the De Turk's divorce official, awarding Mattie $35 a month in alimony.[152]

Still living with his ex-wife two days before Christmas 1914, Joshua De Turk received a summons concerning a Citizens Trust & Savings Bank civil action. Described as "strangely excited" after its delivery, the 81-year-old retired to his bedroom and died within minutes. An employee found his body, and workers removed it to a Hollywood morgue. To her utter dismay, her ex-husband bequeathed Mattie naught but a one-acre lot, which included their home on George Street, valued at $4,500. Joshua left the rest of his estate, including land and stocks in farming and the Wykoff Excavating and Ditching Company, to his sister Esther Amanda Holl of Reading, Pennsylvania. Mattie filed suit in the spring of 1915 to break her former husband's will. It stated that Joshua never used Mattie's money for investment or purchases. Asserting that the estate was community property and not Joshua's separate property, she maintained that patent promoter Habeas Corpus Ladd stood "responsible for cutting [her] off with only one acre of ground." Mattie stated that she contributed money to buy their 14-acre property and to operate the family business. She also contended that Bright's disease (kidney) had clouded J.G.'s mind and rendered him "not competent to execute a will." Estimates of Joshua's estate value placed it between $75,000 and $200,000 ($2,079,313 and $5,544,834 in 2021).[153]

She hurled a "not only cruel but niggardly" charge at her husband's remains. The deceased's attorney declared, "Far from being a weak-minded old man, [or] the victim of a designing promoter… the hog king was shrewd and far-seeing." Los Angeles County Probate Court tossed Mattie's suit when she failed to produce a written copy proving her right to ownership of the Vernon property.[154]

During Mattie's escalating marital troubles, her boy Eddie resided in San Quentin Prison under a seven-year sentence. Steadfast in loyalty to him and a persuasive speaker, Mattie convinced a group of Santa Ana and Los Angeles club and society women to seek a pardon for him. With astonishing success, she won Eddie's parole on March 1, 1915, after he had served less than three years. Back on his immoral track just two months after his release, Eddie pulled his long, green automobile alongside a seven-year-old boy as he walked toward the playground near the Downey Avenue Bridge. He called to the boy, "Come along, sonny. I have got some candy for you and will take you to Pasadena."

"Will you take me through Busch Gardens, too?" replied the lad. "I've heard so much about that beautiful place. If you promise to bring me back home by supper time, I'll go."

Reneging on that promise, Keyes drove deep into the Mojave Desert, where he picked up his red-headed, cave-dwelling friend, Edward "Red" Schaefer. They stayed in an isolated area for three days, and only Schaefer's intervention prevented the child's murder. When the boy returned home, he told the wild tale of traveling through the desert and the horrors of his abduction. As the youngster shared the specifics of the detestable debauchery, Police Chief Charles E. Sebastian suffered "trembles with emotion." He ordered all patrolmen in the city to join the search for his violator.[155]

Arrested for the kidnapping on May 20, 1915, Eddie Keyes disappeared after his mother posted a $3,000 ($83,173 in 2021) bond. Mattie traveled to a northern California mining camp to retrieve Eddie eight months after he fled. He lived as an outlaw on the hog ranch for more than a year until one June 1916 night. While Eddie slept inside the gate leading to Mattie's house, a large posse of city detectives and deputy sheriffs surrounded the De Turk hog ranch. When he issued a loud snore, Detective Burt pounced on him. Mattie then attempted to shoot Deputy Sheriff Sweezy, only to have Burt block her with a swift move.[156]

In court, District Attorney West declared Keyes sane and accused him of using the insanity plea to escape prison. Expert alienist (psychologist) Dr. Don Flagg determined Eddie criminally insane and that "turning him loose on the streets was like loosing a tiger among the people." Flagg's statement and Keyes' delusions, including a claim that he could conquer Mexico with 35–40 bulldogs that he owned, compelled the judge to declare him mentally deranged and commit him to California's Patton State Hospital on August 10, 1916. The consequences for Eddie's evil actions would once again prove insufficient.[157]

21

The Wild Ride Rolls On

Mattie De Turk owned a stylish Willys-Overland touring car in 1915.
(https://www.loc.gov/pictures/item/93513097/)

The emotional soup thickened along the Los Angeles River when Mattie's second husband, J.J. Romig, moved to Vernon around 1914. The former parachuting balloonist first hired on as a foreman with sand and gravel contractors Tieffer & Roach just one block from Mattie's 2600 Twenty-Sixth Street address. Romig then took a job driving a team for Mattie. In April 1915, he wed the De Turk family cook, Birtha Williams. His bride, a native of Norway, held five years over her 53-year-old groom, and Romig's betrothal failed to halt his raucous reverie with Mattie. Four months after their wedding, an intoxicated Romig drove Mattie in her Willys-Overland automobile along Wilshire Boulevard through Santa Monica.

In a sublime inebriation exhibition, the pair created a full-blown street scene. Romig opened festivities when he plowed her car into R.T. Stephens' machine and followed it up by smashing into G.L. Detzer's

(https://www.familysearch.org/ark:/61903/1:1:XLHS-3XX)

vehicle. Sirens screamed as the police ambulance hurried to the wreck before crashing into another auto. Neither Mattie nor her soused "Prof." sustained injuries and, as a ruse to protect Romig's driving privileges, she claimed that she drove the wayward auto, giving his name as H.L. Rigleshuger to police. Incriminating evidence surfaced when license plates from a recently stolen car turned up in Mattie's Overland. Surprisingly, the pair escaped further questioning, and Mattie paid a $50 fine but served no jail time. Romig caught 90 days in jail and a $100 fine for his vehicular depravity.[158]

Her adventures ever newsworthy in a county of more than a half-million people, robust-as-ever Martha De Turk next proved herself "still a man's equal in strength and more than a match in wits," a *Los Angeles Evening Express* writer declared. The tale unfolded "like the scenario of a melodramatic Motion-picture play, with thrills and sensations."[159]

In August 1916, her son Eddie's crazed friend, Red Schaefer, rushed upon her with a large rock. Mattie had recently charged the nefarious ex-cavalryman and cave/mine owner with forging her name on a check. She explained the ensuing insanity, "He was chasing me around the room when I yelled, 'Sic 'im Tige! Grab 'im.' Schaefer thought a dog was going to bite him, but there wasn't any dog. While he was looking for the beast, I knocked the rock out of his hand and jumped out of the room." She then rushed to telephone the Los Angeles County Sheriff's office. Trapped behind the sealed door, Schaefer found an ax and bashed through it. Ever-equal to danger's fiercest fury, Mattie slung pieces of her porcelain china and glassware at Schaefer to keep him at bay until Deputy Sheriffs Rankin and Sweezy arrived to take him to jail. Mattie explained she had not owned a bank account for two years and thus had written no checks. Schaefer soon admitted to creating the valueless check.[160]

Mattie relocated to Newport Beach, California, around May 1917. Believing it a "dry town" and best for her boy Eddie in his war with alcohol, she moved to Lew H. Wallace's "White City Chicken Ranch." After purchasing chickens and a vehicle, she convinced the California State Hospital to release Eddie into her custody. That July, the hospital's log entry regarding Keyes stated, "Discharged. Recovered." Eddie worked picking up garbage at his mother's ranch and the surrounding area to feed the chickens and some hogs. Mattie then ceded the running of the operation to Eddie and gave him money and a checkbook. However, she soon found him making trips to Anaheim, a "wet" community, to buy liquor and sell it to "dry" Newport Beach locals. Eddie later revealed that they paid him with "lots of booze and gasoline, not money." He disappeared that October until a Bedford, Oregon, doctor called saying he had treated Eddie for "an insane condition."[161]

After Eddie returned home, he, Mattie, and an unidentified male driver pulled a car up in front of M. Grazier's general merchandise store in Norwalk, California. In the 2:00 a.m. darkness of November 27, 1917, Mattie remained seated inside while the two men stepped from the vehicle, approached the store, and knocked on the door. Unbeknownst to them, Norwalk had endured a rash of robberies over the last six months, and a Vigilante Committee of "watchers" now guarded the town's post office and other businesses each night. A watchman alerted several "keen-eyed" men, who, armed with rifles, shotguns, and revolvers, presumed that they'd trapped thieves trying to rob the store. Jumping into their car, the suspected trio ignored orders to stop as gunfire crackled in the early morning air. A dozen or more vigilantes raced after them, firing wildly from their vehicles. One man with a repeating shotgun filled the darkness with gunfire, and buckshot blasted into both of Mattie's arms. A half-hour later, authorities located the suspects' automobile abandoned several miles away and Mattie inside the home of J.B. Dean, still bleeding.

Eddie maintained that he and his mother stopped at what they believed was a hotel to find a room. Later, the story changed to them looking to buy groceries. Though convinced of their guilt, the Sheriff's Office soon released the pair for lack of evidence. Months later, law officers continued to insist Mattie's bullet wounds occurred when she attempted to rob the Norwalk store. While she recuperated in the hospital, her case demanding that N.O. Harmon halt removal of sand and gravel from the Vernon acreage came

VIGILANTES SHOOT ELDERLY WOMAN.

HER SON IS ARRESTED AND RELEASED IN CONNECTION WITH NORWALK AFFAIR.

Mrs. Martha de Turk is at the County Hospital suffering from buckshot wounds in both arms, the result of a shooting affair at Nor-

Los Angeles Times, November 28, 1917

before the California State Supreme Court. On December 18, 1917, the court ruled against Mattie. The land where she toiled day upon day—gone! The riverbank where she built her nest egg a few cents at a time—gone! Gone forever![162]

22

Revulsion Outruns Imagination

Mattie's unmitigated repugnance soon one-upped having her arms pumped full of buckshot and Supreme Court losses. America's once high-flying, and now life-trampled, survivor faced the unthinkable. As the late fall's darkness settled over Santa Ana, California, on

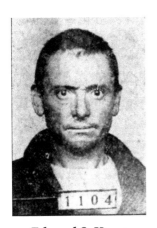

Edward S. Keyes

Santa Ana Register, February 15, 1918

December 7, 1917, two young boys stood on the northwest corner of Bush Street and Washington Avenue selling newspapers. Decked out in a red sweater, Eddie Keyes pulled his small Ford truck up to the corner and lured one of the children into his vehicle by offering him a dollar to ride with him to Anaheim. Taking the boy to his shack on the White City Chicken Ranch, Keyes got him drunk and abused him before choking the child to death and burning his clothes. He then used a butcher knife to decapitate the corpse. Keyes hauled the lifeless body to his truck the next day and dumped it about three miles south of Santa Ana in the Delhi District Drainage Ditch.

He then toted the head toward Santa Ana, where he set it atop a cross timber under the Southern Pacific Railroad bridge. When he arrived to hunt ducks that morning, Villa Park resident Edward Lee came upon the child's headless remains.[163]

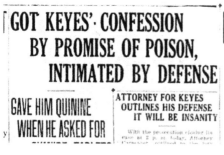

Fresh off his dreadful death-dealing, Eddie returned to Orange County Hospital, where his mother nursed her gunshot wounds. He drove her back to their small ranch, and when they arrived, he began to hemorrhage and spew blood. Mattie called a doctor who ordered Eddie into the hospital, where officers arrested him for the newsboy's murder. Keyes' admitted he killed the child. The killing's details stood so nauseating that hardened law officers, Orange County Sheriff Logan Jackson, and his deputies shuddered at the account. Eddie directed officers to the location of the boy's severed head.[164]

RIFLEMEN GUARD KEYES AGAINST PLAN TO TAKE AND BURN HIM

The *Santa Ana Register* called the killing "the most atrocious in [the] history of Orange County," and news of the murder rushed through town. A lynch mob gathered outside the county jail, and Sheriff Jackson received reports that the mob would "try to take Keys [sic] out and burn him at the stake." He issued his Home Guard officers "shoot to kill" orders to protect Keyes. Armed forces stood guard until Jackson felt "satisfied that the citizens [were] content to let the law take its course." Authorities moved Keyes to the Los Angeles County jail under guard, where he pestered a deputy for cyanide tablets after divulging every gruesome detail of his crime. The officer handed him quinine pills instead. Eddie's attorney argued insanity and the inability to distinguish right from wrong. "The biggest crowd ever in attendance at a criminal trial in Orange County" packed the venue. Still fearing an attempt to lynch him, six policemen escorted the accused into the courtroom.[165]

Prosecutors displayed the murdered child's belt buckle, buttons, and newspaper badge recovered in the ashes of Eddie's stove. Blood found in his vehicle and home, and his directing officers to the corpse's missing head helped confirm Keyes' inhumanity. The killer's confession solidified his guilt, and the case again centered on the question of Eddie's sanity. Mattie drove hard to secure an insanity plea and save her son's life, testifying that Eddie had "lived like a beast for years and committed numerous crimes while under the influence of liquor."

Hoping to indemnify her son against execution, she ended two hours of testimony by saying, "I am positive that he does not realize today what he has done. I have always thought him to be insane. He is insane. He never knew the difference between right and wrong."[166]

District Attorney L.A. West challenged, "You say you always thought your son was insane, yet after he came to the ranch at Newport Beach, you turned this ranch over to him, you put money in the bank for him, and gave him a checkbook?" Eddie lounged in his chair, appearing disinterested and near sleep throughout the legal exercise, even as the jury endured listening to his horrifying account of killing and beheading the victim.[167]

Eddie's attorney declared his confession "merely the outcropping of the mind of a half-witted man." Supporting evidence came from

Dr. Allen, who proclaimed Eddie a moron—a man physically, but with the mind of a child of 9 or 10 years old and unable to distinguish between right and wrong. District Attorney West explained that officers had "long known" Eddie as a "degenerate, afflicted with moral degeneration, but not mental degeneration." The killer then flipped an emotional switch. "When the jury went out, he brightened up and discussed the probable verdict." The gut-wrenching predator predicted, "They'll hang me."[168]

People stood on tables and chairs awaiting the verdict in the packed courtroom and Keyes' reaction. "In no trial in this county has the attendance been greater," declared the *Register's* court reporter. After less than 40 minutes of deliberation, the jury foreman delivered the guilty-of-first-degree murder verdict, with death as its penalty. Eddie slowly finished rolling a cigarette and smiled before licking its edge and proclaiming to Deputy A.E. Koepsel, "I don't give a damn. I expected it." Walking back to his cell, he added, "If they thought I was going to cry, they were damn badly mistaken."[169]

Traveling to San Quentin for his scheduled April 19, 1918 hanging, Keyes confessed to at least three additional murders. Orange County Sheriff Logan Jackson reported, "He told me he brained a man in Los Angeles and robbed him of $160." Eddie also stated that he and his friend Red Schaefer attempted to burglarize the house of a man named Baker in Ventura County in May 1916. While Keyes stood guard outside, Schaefer shot and killed Baker when he surprised him. Jackson verified Keyes' story with the local sheriff, which quieted those who felt his record, "marked by a decided streak of degeneracy and insanity," made the confession "practically worthless."[170]

In the meantime, his attorney appealed the court's sanity ruling, staying Eddie's execution. His case reached the California Supreme Court, which upheld the earlier court's finding. Scheduled to hang on December 20, 1918, Edward S. Keyes returned to Orange County jail, where he contracted pneumonia. Authorities transported him to the Santa Ana County Hospital, where he died of pneumonia and the Spanish Flu on October 23, 1918, at 29. The *Santa Ana Register* announced his demise, saying, "Hangman Cheated by Death: Murder Most Ferocious in County's History." The crime stood as "the most brutal in the history of Orange County," and the hanging, had it occurred, would have been the first resulting from a conviction in Orange County.[171]

GALLOWS CHEATED WHEN INFLUENZA CLAIMS VICTIM

Special Dispatch to Evening Express

SANTA ANA, Oct. 23.—Under sentence to be hanged on December 20

Los Angeles Evening Express, October 23, 1918

Santa Ana Register, December 17, 1917

23

True Grit 'til the End, No Matter Her Name

T he death of her beloved boy and his vicious crimes surely crushed Mattie emotionally, yet it failed to define her. Many specifics of her life went unreported subsequently, but she endured another 22 years. The City of Vernon named Mattie in a lawsuit in 1921. It demanded that she, her late husband Joshua, and others remove a 420-foot-long by 70-foot-wide pile of rubbish, tin cans, and other refuse in the Los Angeles River bed. "In time, [the trash pile would] divert the channel of the river and also damage a bridge built by the city," claimed officials. Reports of the outcome of this suit remain at large.[172]

The 1926 Los Angeles City Directory showed Mattie living in the old De Turk home at 2600 Twenty-Sixth Street in Vernon. Four years later, 1930 U.S. Census records reported 68-year-old James J. Romig, her aerial Professor, former husband, and playmate living with Mattie as her sole roomer. Speculation points to the explosive pair spending their last years together in San Diego, where Romig died on September 20, 1937. The 1938 San Diego City Directory listed Mattie as living at 3552 4th Avenue.[173]

That January, the court found the formidable woman incapable of managing her personal affairs and appointed a guardian, most likely her daughter-in-law Cassie Keyes. She took charge of Mattie's $20,000 estate, probably built through the sale of her Vernon home. Ever ready for the next round, Mattie fought the ruling in August 1938. After deliberating just 10 minutes, a jury ruled her able "to care for herself and her savings." Records next showed her living with Cassie Keyes in Alpine, California, in the mountains east of San Diego.

PIONEER WOMAN PARACHUTE JUMPER RULED COMPETENT

San Diego Union, August 16, 1938

The 1940 U.S. Census listed Martha H. "Mattie" De Turk as a "patient" in San Diego's Hillcrest Home for the Aged at 4004 Vermont Street. Suffering from senility and, for the last three months of her life, pemphigus, an autoimmune disease resulting in blisters and sores on the skin, she died in the Hillcrest Home on August 24, 1940. Despite the lack of "causative history," valvular heart disease of an "undetermined" duration contributed to her death.[174]

Miss Hazel Keyes/Mattie H. De Turk lived a whirlwind life that transcended the mundane, surmounted the unusual, and overcame the extraordinary to crest somewhere beyond stunning and astonishing and stand atop the unfathomable. Diving dirtward with enduring hope of an air-filled parachute and painless descent, Miss Hazel played fast, rough, and loose with her body for a stash of cash and a spot of fame. Retiring from an often brutal parachuting career, she battled "the powers" and her last husband to build and maintain wealth and local renown as Los Angeles' Sand-Lot Queen. While some might question her maternal skills, her motherly love stood obvious. Her sons remained dear to her into their adulthood, despite stealing from her and wreaking chaos in her life. Demanding honesty, however, she pressed charges against them when deserved.

This narrative reflects one soul's sensational saga and her transition from sky to turf through repeated and unfathomable physical and emotional challenges. Questions arise as to which events in such a variable, multi-dimensional existence molded this amazing soul. That the day's newspapers followed her activities for so many years proves remarkable and provides a unique window into her life's bright and dismal corners. However, discerning more regarding her nature falls outside our ability to recoup the ages. For truth's sake, naught but conjecture and further investigation will wield the brush that finishes Miss Hazel Keyes' lifescape.

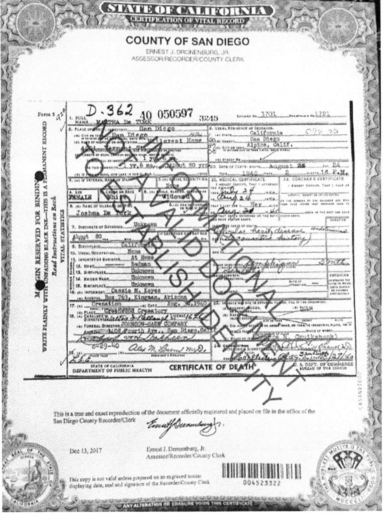

(California Department of Health)

Endnotes

1. trtworld.com, TRTWORLD, "Abbas Ibn Firnas: The First Human to Fly"; *juliantrubin.com,* "Leonardo da Vinci: The Invention of the Parachute"; scienceource.com; tourdalmatia.com, "Croatian Inventor of the Parachute."

2. Charles A. Lindbergh, inspiringquotes.us.

3. *Arizona Republican* (Phoenix), January 27, 1895, "In Mid-Air: Death Grinned at Two Clinging Aeronauts."

4. *San Francisco Chronicle,* January 31, 1887, "A Thrilling Descent."

5. digital.sciencehistory.org/works/3197xm10p; Tom D. Crouch, *The Eagle Aloft: Two Centuries of the Balloon in America,* Smithsonian Institution Press, Washington, D.C., 1983, p. 475.

6. *Los Angeles Times,* July 27, 1888, "That Big Jump."

7. *globasecurity.com;* berlin-airport.de; Gary B. Fogel and Craig S. Harwood, *Quest for Flight: John J. Montgomery and the Dawn of Aviation in the West,* University of Oklahoma Press, Norman, 2012, p. 70; *Richard T. Read and David Rambow, Hydrogen and Smoke: A Survey of Lighter-Than-Air Flight in South Dakota Prior to World War I. South Dakota Historical Society Press, Pierre, vol. 18(3): Fall 1988, P. 133–136. (https://www.sdhspress.com/journal/south-dakota-history-18-3/hydrogen-and-smoke-a-survey-of-lighter-than-air-flight-in-south-dakota-prior-to-world-war-i/).*

8. 1870 U.S. Census, Los Nietos Township, California; 1880 U.S Census records, Multnomah County, Oregon; Note: William Horton (1835–ca. 1913), Mary Adeline Redmond (1843–??); Martha Horton (Hazel Keyes)

listed as six years old—later records indicate her birth date as 1861; 2021 inflation figures—https://westegg.com/inflation/.

9. *Oregon Daily Statesman* (Salem), August 15, 1886, "Sued for Damages"; October 16, 1886, "Dismissed—Disappointed."

10. *Morning Oregonian* (Portland), August 14, 1886, "Local and General: Damage Suit"; September 14, 1886, "Personal: Assault of a Woman."

11. *Morning Oregonian* (Portland), December 9, 1886, "Personal: Another Suit for Damages"; December 16, 1886, "Police Court."

12. *Oregon Daily Statesman* (Salem), July 14, 1887, "Suit Between Lawyers"; *Morning Oregonian* (Portland), March 26, 1887, "Reversal of Damage Suit"; June 14, 1887, "Keyes vs. Baker."

13. *Oregon Daily Statesman* (Salem), September 3, 1897, "Building a Balloon."

14. *Oakland Tribune,* January 17, 1890, "Necrology"; *Spokane Falls Review* (Washington), May 31, 1890, "In the Home Field." Note: The Keyes home stood at 523 Sixteenth Street in Oakland.

15. *The Daily Morning Astorian* (Astoria, Oregon), August 14, 1890, "Did He Commit Suicide?"; *San Francisco Chronicle,* August 11, 1890, "An Aeronaut's Death." Note: C.P. Redmond died near Snohomish, Washington, in May 1890.

16. Ibid.

17. *The Daily Morning Astorian* (Astoria, Oregon), July 21, 1890, "Up in a Balloon."; *Morning Daily Herald* (Albany, Oregon), September 11, 1890, "Jottings About Town"; *Oregon Daily Statesman* (Salem), September 3, 1897, "Building a Balloon"; *Evening Capital Journal* (Salem, Oregon), September 1, 1890, "Double Parachute Jump at Gervais."

18. *Washington Times* (Washington, D.C.), April 23, 1894, "Falling from a Balloon"; *Weekly Oregon Statesman* (Salem), November 3, 1893, "Up in a Balloon Boys."

19. *The Saint Paul Globe* (Minnesota), August 20, 1899, "Life and Death Struggles in the Clouds."

20. *Chicago Tribune,* August 16, 1891, "Killed by a Fall from a Balloon."

21. *The Pittsburgh Press,* September 19, 1899, "Parachute Mortality"; *Meade County Press-Democrat* (Kansas), November 30, 1888, "A Balloonist Drowned"; *Detroit Free Press,* August 31, 1891, "An Awful Plunge"; *The Atlanta Constitution,* July 6, 1890, "His Last Jump"; *San Francisco Examiner,* August 2, 1894, "Fell from a Parachute"; *Logansport Reporter* (Indiana), August 2, 1894, "Better Quit It, Boys."

22. *Sioux City Journal* (Iowa), October 2, 1898, "An Aeronaut Killed"; *Marengo Republican News* (Illinois), August 5, 1892, "The News Condensed."

23. *The Scranton Tribune* (Pennsylvania), July 10, 1897, "Untitled"; *The Buffalo Times* (New York), August 20, 1891, "Editorial Jottings."

24. *The Morning Call* (San Francisco), November 17, 1890, "Balloon Ascension."

25. Ibid.

26. *Oakland Tribune,* February 3, 1891, "Up in a Balloon"; *Humboldt Times* (California), March 20, 1891, "Did You See the Balloon."

27. *Blue Lake Advocate* (California), March 28, 1891, "McGinty's Letter."

28. *Sacramento Daily Record-Union,* April 13, 1891, "Yesterday's Ascension"; *Oakland Tribune,* June 22, 1891, "Proceeds of a Perilous Trip"; *The Morning Call* (San Francisco), June 26, 1891, "A Wonderful Feat"; https://westegg.com/inflation/.

29. *The Morning Call* (San Francisco), June 14, 1891, "Laundry Farm"; June 19, 1891, "A Jump from the Clouds"; June 26, 1891, "A Wonderful Feat"; *Sacramento Daily Record-Union,* April 11, 1891, "The Balloon Ascension"; *San Francisco Examiner,* June 22, 1891, "Up in a Balloon"; *Oakland Tribune,* June 29, 1891, "At Laundry Farm."

30. *San Francisco Examiner,* June 10, 1891, "Robbed His Employer"; October 24, 1891, "Keyes Bonds Forfeited."

31. *San Francisco Examiner,* October 23, 1891, "Police Court Trickery"; October 24, 1891, "Keyes Bond Forfeited"; *The Morning Call* (San Francisco), October 24, 1891, "Crookedness in Court"; October 23, 1891, "Who Is Responsible?"

32. *San Francisco, Chronicle,* July 5, 1891, "Keeping the Fourth."

33. *Los Angeles Herald,* August 1, 1891, "Santa Monica."

34. *Los Angeles Herald,* August 31, 1891, "At the Beaches"; *The Daily Intelligencer* (Wheeling, West Virginia), September 8, 1891, "Untitled."

35. *The Morning Call* (San Francisco), September 17, 1891, "The State Fair"; September 20, 1891, "The Last Day at Sacramento"; *Sacramento Daily Record-Union,* September 19, 1891, "Last Day of the Fair: Today's Events."

36. *Sacramento Daily Record-Union,* September 15, 1891, "At the Park."

37. Ibid.

38. *Los Angeles Herald,* October 18, 1891, "Up in a Balloon"; *Weekly Oregon Statesman* (Salem), November 3, 1893, "Up in a Balloon Boys."

39. *Los Angeles Herald,* October 18, 1891, "Up in a Balloon"; *San Diego Union & Daily Bee,* December 9, 1891, "Local Intelligence."

40. *San Francisco Examiner,* February 19, 1893, "Two Gifted Monkies."

41. *Weekly Oregon Statesman* (Salem), November 3, 1893, "Up in a Balloon Boys"; *Los Angeles Herald,* February 20, 1892, "Miss Keyes' Monkey."

42. Ibid.

43. *Sacramento Daily Record-Union,* March 21, 1892, "The Balloon Soared Alone."

44. *The Seattle Post-Intelligencer,* July 25, 1892, "Sailing Into the Sky."

45. *The Seattle Post-Intelligencer,* August 15, 1892, "Dragged on Fence."

46. Ibid; *The Morning Call* (San Francisco), August 17, 1892, "Miss Keyes the Aeronaut Recovering"; *The Seattle Post-Intelligencer,* August 28, 1892, "It Was a Great Day"; *Santa Cruz Sentinel* (California), October 2, 1892, "San Jose Fair"; *San Jose Mercury-News]* (California), October 1, 1892, "A Perilous Fall."

47. *San Francisco Chronicle,* May 13, 1893, "She Courted Death."

48. *San Francisco Chronicle,* April 17, 1893, "A Bride's Balloon"; April 30, 1893, "Plucky as Ever."

49. *San Francisco Chronicle,* May 18, 1893, "To the Tomb."

50. *San Francisco Examiner,* May 14, 1893, "Grave-Robbers Detected."

51. *San Francisco Examiner,* June 5, 1893, "Rescued from the Masts."

52. *San Francisco Chronicle,* June 5, 1893, "Flew Through Space"; *San Francisco Examiner,* June 5, 1893, "Rescued from the Masts."

53. *The Morning Call* (San Francisco), June 5, 1893, "Hung on a Yard"; *Sausalito News* (Sausalito, California), June 9, 1893, "A Mid-Air Adventure"; *San Francisco Chronicle,* June 5, 1893, "Flew Through Space."

54. *The Morning Call* (San Francisco), June 5, 1893, "Hung on a Yard."

55. Ibid; *Sausalito News* (Sausalito, California), June 9, 1893, "A Mid-Air Adventure."

56. *Sausalito News* (Sausalito, California), June 9, 1893, "A Mid-Air Adventure."

57. *San Francisco Chronicle,* June 5, 1893, "She Lands in the Rigging of a Ship"; *The Topeka Daily Press* (Kansas), June 26, 1893, "An Acrobatic Aeronaut"; *Akron Daily Democrat* (Ohio), June 24, 1893, "An Acrobatic Aeronaut"; *Buffalo Evening News* (New York), June 23, 1892, "An Acrobatic Aeronaut"; *The Morning News* (Wilmington, Delaware), June 23, 1893, "An Acrobatic Aeronaut"; *The News* (Frederick, Maryland), June 30, 1893, "An Acrobatic Aeronaut."

58. *The Seattle Post-Intelligencer*, July 24, 1893, "Fun with a Monkey."

59. Ibid.

60. Ibid.

61. *The Seattle Post-Intelligencer,* July 26, 1893, "Will Not Prosecute the Aeronaut."

62. *Washington Standard* (Olympia), August 25, 1893, "A Soar in Cloudland."

63. Ibid.

64. Ibid.

65. *Weekly Oregon Statesman* (Salem), November 3, 1893, "Up in a Balloon Boys."

66. Ibid.

67. *Oregon Evening Capital Journal* (Salem), October 25, 1893, "Free Balloon"; October 30, 1893, "Second Balloon Ascension"; November 6, 1893, "Mid-Air Money Robbery"; "The Woman Aerialist Held Up at the State Fair Grounds"; https://westegg.com/inflation/.

68. Ibid. Note: Rumors reported in Salem's *Weekly Oregon Statesman* of Miss Jennie Yan Yan's December 1893 death in California went unsubstantiated. Salem's Fairgrounds sat on the Savage-Rideout property.

69. *Weekly Oregon Statesman* (Salem), November 10, 1893, "Yesterday's Ballooning."

70. *Sacramento Daily Record-Union,* January 8, 1894, "A Woman's Curiosity"; *The Morning Call* (San Francisco), January 8, 1894, "She Looked the Wrong Way."

71. *Los Angeles Herald,* May 14, 1894, "A Violent Balloonist."

72. Ibid.

73. Ibid; *Los Angeles Herald,* May 15, 1894, "Failed to Appear."

74. *La Jolla Light* (California), April 17, 2019, "'Chuting Star'"; *La Jolla Historical Society* "Timekeeper," Spring/Summer 2019; "Who's Who in Ballooning," balloonhistory.com; *San Diego Union,* June 11, 1894, "The Balloon Ascension"; June 17, 1894, "The Balloon Ascent"; *Los Angeles Herald,* September 12, 1894, "The Benson Benefit."

75. *The Times Herald* (Port Huron, Michigan), February 7, 1894, "Jumping from a Balloon."

76. Ibid.

77. *Arizona Sentinel* (Yuma), November 24, 1894, "Local Briefs"; *The Oasis* (Arizola, Arizona), December 6, 1894, "Arizona News."

78. *Arizona Republican* (Phoenix), March 15, 1895, "Local Briefs"; March 17, 1895, "Local Briefs." Note: Other reports stated that the balloon reached 2000–3,000 feet.

79. *Oregon Daily Statesman* (Salem), February 17, 1895, "Hazel Keyes in Peril"; *Arizona Republican* (Phoenix), March 19, 1895, "This Time by Fire."

80. *Mohave County Miner* (Mineral Park, Arizona), July 6, 1895, "Simpson & Hack Fruit Company."

81. *Arizona Kicker, Tombstone Epitaph* (Arizona), September 29, 1895, "Stabbed a Woman."

82. Ibid; *Arizona Republican* (Phoenix), September 26, 1895, "Local Briefs"; October 5, 1895, "All Over Arizona"; *Arizona Sentinel* (Yuma), September 28, 1895, "Local News."

83. *Dakota County Record* (South Sioux City, Nebraska), September 12, 1896, "His Wife Protested"; *St. Joseph Weekly Gazette* (Missouri), September 18, 1896, "Chief's Bluff"; *Copper Country Evening News* (Calumet,

Michigan), September 17, 1896, "Will Rise in Balloons"; *Sioux City Journal* (Iowa), August 30, 1896, "Jottings About Town: News Briefs."

84. *St. Joseph Weekly Gazette* (Missouri), September 18, 1896, "Chief's Bluff"; *Dakota County Record* (South Sioux City, Nebraska), September 19, 1896, "All the Local News"; *North Nebraska Eagle* (Dakota City), September 17, 1896, "Dakota County Mention."

85. *The Chanute Daily Tribune* (Kansas), September 18, 1896, "Post Office Clerk's Officers"; *St. Joseph Weekly Gazette* (Missouri), September 16, 1896, "Chief's Bluff"; *Boston Globe*, September 20, 1896, in *Harper's Weekly*, October 6, 1896, "Inventions."

86. *Argus Leader* (Sioux Falls, South Dakota), September 23, 1896, "The Great Fair"; *Lincoln Evening Call* (Nebraska), October 9, 1896, "Brevities."

87. *The Birmingham News* (Alabama), June 7, 1897, "It Didn't Work"; *Birmingham State Herald* (Alabama), June 8, 1897, "Thrilling Experience"; *Chattanooga Daily Times* (Tennessee), August 28, 1897, "A Novel Entertainment." Note: Robert Warnock, Thomas Jones, and John Connelly rescued Miss Hazel.

88. *Austin Daily Statesman* (Texas), July 12, 1898, "A Man Wanted."

89. *Austin Daily Statesman* (Texas), July 17, 1898, "The Lake Excursion"; August 29, 1898, "Yesterday's Ascension."

90. Ibid.

91. Ibid.

92. Ibid. Note: Miss Hazel's rescuers included Ben Alexander, Frank Bliss, and Curtis Tuemey.

93. *Austin Daily Statesman* (Texas), September 4, 1898, "Suspended by Her Hair"; September 5, 1898, "Much Bravery Displayed."

94. *Austin Daily Statesman* (Texas), September 4, 1898, "Balloon Ascension"; October 15, 1898, "At the Dam Sunday"; June 16, 1899, "Bits of City News"; https://readtheplaque.com/plaque/mount-bonnell.

95. *Austin Daily Statesman* (Texas), October 1, 1899, "Brief Bits of City News"; *Fort Worth Record and Register* (Texas), December 9, 1899, "Theatrical World"; *Houston Post* (Texas), August 3, 1900, "Reunion at Dublin"; *The Copper Era and Morenci Leader* (Clifton, Arizona), November 1, 1900, "Untitled."

96. *Graham Guardian* (Safford, Arizona), December 7, 1900, "The Ascension." Note: The same article tells of 1000 to 2000-foot estimates.

97. Ibid; *The Graham County Guardian* (Safford, Arizona), December 7, 1900, "The Kid Skipped."

98. *Arizona Weekly Journal-Miner* (Prescott), June 28, 1901, "Renowned Aeronaut"; June 29, 1901, "A Monster Air Ship"; June 28, 1901, "Renowned Aeronaut."

99. *Arizona Weekly Journal-Miner* (Prescott), July 10, 1901, "The Eagle Screamed."

100. *Arizona Weekly Journal-Miner* (Prescott), July 10, 1901, "Miss Hazel Keyes' Aerial Voyage"; July 10, 1901, "Saturday Night's Ascension"; *Arizona Republican* (Phoenix), July 10, 1901, "News of the North: Prescott."

101. *Arizona Weekly Journal-Miner* (Prescott), July 10, 1901, "Local News."

102. Complaint #3387, James J. Romig vs. Martha H. Romig, August 29, 1901, Yavapai County Fourth Judicial District Court.

103. Ibid.

104. Complaint #3465, Martha H. Romig vs. James J. Romig, February 14, 1902, Yavapai County Fourth Judicial District Court.

105. R.N. Copeland deposition, Yavapai County Fourth Judicial District Court, March 31, 1902; Complaint #3465 Martha H. Romig vs. James J. Romig, February 14, 1902, Fourth Judicial District, Yavapai County District Court.

106. Doubletree—a crossbar in front of a wagon with a swingletree (a crossbar pivoted in the middle, where the traces attach in a horse-drawn wagon or plow; a singletree) at each end, enabling two horses to be harnessed abreast.

107. *Los Angeles Times,* November 2, 1882, "Another Runaway."

108. *Los Angeles Herald*, October 19, 1880, "Local Brevities."

109. *Los Angeles Herald,* May 27, 1883, "Advertisement"; September 22, 1880, "Local Brevities"; November 1, 1893, "Property Transfers"; August 8, 1884, "Untitled"; November 9, 1883, "Society Notices"; *Los Angeles Times*, September 27, 1887, "The Odd Fellows."

110. *Los Angeles Times*, May 6, 1885, "The City"; April 23, 1890, "The Courts: Sensational Divorce Case"; *Los Angeles Herald*, April 23, 1890, "The De Turk Divorce."

111. *Los Angeles Times*, May 29, 1898, "The Flag Cottage"; April 23, 1890, "The Courts: Sensational Divorce Case."

112. *Los Angeles Times*, September 16, 1887, "A Big Buy"; April 23, 1890, "The Courts: Sensational Divorce Case"; October 29, 1898, "A Costly Divorce"; June 2, 1892, "Big Board Bill"; October 29, 1898, "A Fatal Defect Found"; *Los Angeles Herald*, October 13, 1897, "Odd Contract"; *Los Angeles Times*, December 30, 1891, "Real Estate Transfers." Note: Hartensteins' home stood at 20 N. Fort St. They made improvements, including $525 in trees, etc., and $420 in labor after signing the contract with J.G. De Turk.

113. *Los Angeles Evening Post*, June 4, 1898, "City Briefs." Note: De Turk joined Odd Fellows Lodge #35 on December 21, 1881, at 48. He served a term as the Lodge's Noble Grand until July 1, 1883, and the Lodge suspended him on December 22, 1897, possibly for not paying dues. Correspondence with Gary Carpentier, Noble Grand Los Angeles-Golden Rule Lodge #35, October 13, 2021.

114. *Los Angeles Herald*, February 15, 1899, "De Turk's Troubles"; *Los Angeles Times*, February 15, 1899, "Swill or Garbage?"

115. *Los Angeles Times*, March 19, 1904, "Real Estate Transfers"; March 21, 1909, "Wins Wealth from Rubbish."

116. Ibid; *Los Angeles Times*, May 14, 1915, "Their Trials and Tribulations"; April 7, 1904, "Marriage Licenses"; February 15, 1899, "Swill or Garbage?"; June 22, 1914, "Sand Trail to Night Shooter"; State of California Marriage License, recorded April 12, 1904, in Los Angeles County, by County Recorder. Mattie uses the spelling Roemig on the marriage certificate. This differs from the spelling commonly reported during her parachuting days, Romig.

117. *Los Angeles Times*, March 9, 1913, "This Sand Bank Real Gold Mine."

118. *Los Angeles Times*, March 21, 1909, "Wins Wealth from Rubbish."

119. *Los Angeles Herald*, June 24, 1906, "Babies Devour Garbage"; *Los Angeles Times*, March 21, 1909, "Wins Wealth from Rubbish."

120. *Los Angeles Times,* June 26, 1904, "Negroes on Rampage."

121. *Los Angeles Times,* September 21, 1906, "Trail of Slayer Crosses Country"; *Los Angeles Herald,* August 10, 1906, "Murder Mystery Still Unsolved"; August 12, 1906, "Seek to Identify Canyon Victim."

122. *Los Angeles Herald,* August 16, 1906, "Perhaps Horton's Fiancée."

123. *Los Angeles Herald,* October 10, 1908, "Supreme Court Denies Besold's Appeal"; November 8, 1906, "Women Who Claim to Have Been Wooed and Wedded by the Butcher."

124. *Los Angeles Herald,* December 12, 1907, "City Trustee Is Arrested."

125. Ibid.

126. *Los Angeles Times,* June 3, 1908, "Mother Is in Awful Doubt."

127. Ibid.

128. *Santa Ana Register* (California), February 7, 1918, "Mother Says Keyes Told Her He Found Boy Dead Then Cut Off His Head."

129. Ibid.

130. *Los Angeles Times,* May 14, 1915, "Their Trials and Tribulations."

131. Ibid.

132. Ibid; *Los Angeles Times,* May 15, 1915, "End Mystery?"

133. *Los Angeles Times,* March 21, 1909, "Wins Wealth from Rubbish."

134. *Los Angeles Herald,* October 25, 1909, "Claims Refuse Dump Nuisance."

135. *The Morning Call* (San Francisco), November 17, 1909, "Wanted in Los Angeles to Answer for Theft"; *Los Angeles Herald,* November 20, 1909, "Charged with Stealing Money from His Mother"; Proverb 28:24, Christian Standard Bible.

136. *Los Angeles Herald,* November 20, 1909, "Charged with Stealing Money from His Mother"; November 17, 1909, "Wanted in Los Angeles to Answer For Theft"; *Los Angeles Times,* February 24, 1910, "Conflicting: Bringing Out Queer Facts."

137. *The Morning Call* (San Francisco), May 29, 1910, "Youth Ruined by Spell of Siren"; *San Francisco Examiner,* May 29, 1910, "Sent to Panama as Punishment." Note: Sailing records to the Canal Zone fail to report Joseph Keyes' arrival but show Edward S. Keyes arriving in Panama in mid-April 1910, before Joseph's sentencing. Eddie served as a fireman on a steam shovel before departing the Isthmus after just four months.

138. *Los Angeles Herald,* March 5, 1910, "Keyes Freed of Murder Charge."

139. *Los Angeles Times,* February 23, 1910, "Kills Man He Says He Would Go to Hell For."

140. *Los Angeles Herald,* February 28, 1910, "Murder Charge Filed Against Ed. S. Keyes"; February 25, 1910, "Fatal Shooting During Quarrel Due to Accident"; *Los Angeles Times,* February 23, 1910, "Kills Man He Says He Would Go to Hell For."

141. *Los Angeles Herald,* February 28, 1910, "Murder Charge Filed Against Ed. S. Keyes"; March 3, 1910, "Man Charged with Murder Out on Bail." Note: Attorney Frank Allander represented Eddie. The 1910 U.S. Census shows only Eddie living with Mattie and Joshua. Her older sons Joseph and Henry remained in their mother's life.

142. *Sacramento Star,* November 6, 1911, "Romig Killed by Freight Car"; November 8, 1911, "Death Still a Mystery"; *Sacramento Daily Record-Union,* November 6, 1911, "Heir to Wealth Killed by Train."

143. *Los Angeles Times,* November 25, 1911, "Woman Rancher Halts Garbage Removal Plan."

144. Ibid.

145. *Los Angeles Herald,* March 5, 1910, "Keyes Freed of Murder Charge"; *Los Angeles Times,* April 10, 1912, "Faints in Court."

146. *Los Angeles Times,* June 13, 1914, "A Woman's Home Is Her Castle"; September 29, 1914, "Trial Set"; December 11, 1914, "Garbage Dump Commissariat"; December 29, 1914, "Sand Queen Loser in Will"; *Los Angeles Herald,* December 28, 1914, "Queen of Sand Lot in Will Gets Home."

147. *Los Angeles Times,* June 22, 1914, "Sand Trail to Night Shooter"; June 19, 1914, "Hears Bullets Whistle Through Her Hat." Note: The ranch's most significant sandpit reportedly contained quicksand for the first 2½ feet, followed by 5 feet of brick sand, 25 feet of gravel and sand used for flooring, 4 feet of pea gravel, and 5 feet of silky sand above other strata.

148. *Los Angeles Times,* June 19, 1914, "Old Tin Cans Price of Life."

149. *Los Angeles Times,* September 18, 1914, "Sand Lot Queen Is Hazel Keyes."

150. Ibid; *Los Angeles Herald,* December 23, 1891, "Real Estate Transfers."

151. *Los Angeles Times,* May 14, 1915, "Their Trials and Tribulations."

152. *Los Angeles Times,* July 14, 1914, "Court Restrains Both"; December 11, 1914, "Garbage Dump Commissariat"; *Los Angeles Herald,* May 14, 1915, "Oil Can Bank Is Told in Will Case."

153. *Los Angeles Times,* December 24, 1914, "Gets Last Summons"; December 29, 1914, "At the Courthouse: Sand Queen Is Loser by Will"; December 31, 1914, "Sand Lot Queen"; May 25, 1915, "Argue Contest for De Turk Estate."

154. *Los Angeles Times,* May 26, 1915, "Thrown Out"; December 11, 1914, "Garbage Dump Commissariat"; December 31, 1914, "Sand Lot Queen."

155. *Los Angeles Evening Record,* May 15, 1915, "Tramp Lured Boy, 7, Belied"; *Los Angeles Times,* May 19, 1915, "As a Lamb Is Led to Slaughter."

156. *The Pomona Express* (California), May 21, 1915, "Suspected of Kidnapping"; *Long Beach Telegram* (California), May 20, 1915, "Booked on Suspicion"; *Los Angeles Times,* June 26, 1916, "Snore Betrays"; https://westegg.com/inflation/.

157. *Los Angeles Evening Express,* February 8, 1918, "Alienist Testifies Keyes Was Insane"; *Los Angeles Times,* December 20, 1916, "Pathetic: Woman's Plea Moves to Pity"; *Santa Ana Register* (California), January 24, 1918, "At the Courthouse: Contest of Keyes' Sanity Now Raised."

158. *Los Angeles Times,* August 31, 1915, "Five Autos Wrecked in Santa Monica"; September 1, 1915, "Sand-Lot Queen Fined at Beach: Man Who Drove Her Car into Others Gets Jail Term."

159. *Los Angeles Evening Express,* November 2, 1916, "Woman Tells of Midnight Attack."

160. *Los Angeles Times,* August 13, 1916, "Battle Is Won by Sand-Lot Queen"; November 4, 1916, "His Explanation Was a Boomerang."

161. *Santa Ana Register* (California), December 10, 1917, "Confesses Fiendish Murder of Boy"; February 7, 1918, "Mother Says Keyes Told Her He Found Boy Dead Then Cut Off His Head"; February 7, 1918, "Mrs. De Turk Says She Always Knew Keyes Was Insane";

February 11, 1918, "Evidence in Keyes Case Presented in Brief Form"; January 24, 1918, "Contest Over Keyes' Sanity Waged Now"; February 6, 1918, "Got Keyes Confession by Promise of Poison, Intimated by Defense."

162. *Los Angeles Times,* November 28, 1917, "Vigilantes Shoot Elderly Woman"; *Los Angeles Evening News,* November 29, 1917, "Woman Shot: Mistaken for Burglar in Norwalk Store"; December 19, 1917, "'Sand-Lot Queen' Loses Appeal to Higher Court."

163. *Santa Ana Register* (California), December 10, 1917, "Confesses Fiendish Murder of Boy"; February 6, 1918, "Newsboy Positive Keyes Is Man Who Took Leonard Away"; February 11, 1918, "Evidence in Keyes Case Presented in Brief Form"; *Los Angeles Times,* December 10, 1917, "Arrest Man as Youth's Slayer."

164. *Los Angeles Times,* December 10, 1917, "Arrest Man as Youth's Slayer."

165. *Santa Ana Register* (California), December 28, 1917, "Insanity Plea Keyes's Defense"; December 17, 1917, "Murder of Leonard Hervick Ranks as Most Atrocious in History of Orange County"; *Los Angeles Times,* December 31, 1917, "Threaten to Lynch Keyes"; December 10, 1917, "Arrest Man as Youth's Slayer"; December 31, 1917, "Riflemen Guard Keyes Against Plan to Take and Burn Him"; February 6, 1918, "Got Keyes Confession by Promise of Poison, Intimated by Defense"; February 8, 1918, "Grim Swap to Beat Gallows"; *Feather River Bulletin* (Quincy, California), December 13, 1917, "Horrible Crime."

166. *Los Angeles Times,* December 28, 1917, "Insanity Plea Keyes's Defense"; *Santa Ana Register* (California), December 10, 1917, "Confesses Fiendish Murder of Boy"; February 6, 1918, "Got Keyes Confession by Promise of Poison, Intimated by Defense."

167. *Santa Ana Register* (California), February 7, 1918, "Mother Says Keyes Told Her He Found Boy Dead Then Cut Off His Head"; February 7, 1918, "Mrs. De Turk Says She Always Knew Keyes Was Insane."

168. *Los Angeles Times,* December 28, 1917, "Insanity Plea Keyes's Defense"; February 12, 1918, "Keyes Grins as Jury Says He Is to Hang"; *Santa*

Ana Register (California), February 8, 1918, "Got Keyes Confession by Promise of Poison, Intimated by Defense."

169. Ibid.

170. *Los Angeles Times,* February 24, 1918, "Four Other Murders 'Confessed' by Keyes"; *Bakersfield Californian,* April 22, 1918, "Man Confesses to 3 Unsolved Murders"; *Santa Ana Register* (California), February 23, 1918, "Keyes Says He Brained Man, Robbed Him of $160."

171. Ibid; *Santa Ana Register* (California), October 23, 1918, "Keyes Is Dead of Pneumonia, Body to Be Cremated"; *Los Angeles Times,* October 24, 1918, "Not One Hanged in Thirty Years."

172. *Los Angeles Times,* December 22, 1921, "City Sues Estate."

173. 1926 Los Angeles City Directory, p. 761; 1930 U.S. Census, San Antonio Township, Vernon City, Sheet 6B; 1938 San Diego City Directory, p. 175.

174. *San Diego Union,* August 16, 1938, "Pioneer Woman Parachute Jumper Ruled Competent"; San Diego, California County unofficial death record; 1940 U.S. Federal Population Census, San Diego, Ward 2, Hillcrest Home for the Aged, Sheet 8A.

Ingram Content Group UK Ltd.
Milton Keynes UK
UKHW020910140623
423423UK00011B/422